THE
AMERICAN
CHILD

ELIZABETH McCRACKEN

1st WORLD
LIBRARY
Literary Society

The American Child

Elizabeth McCracken

© 1st World Library – Literary Society, 2005
PO Box 2211
Fairfield, IA 52556
www.1stworldlibrary.org
First Edition

LCCN: 2005906471

Softcover ISBN: 1-4218-1527-3
Hardcover ISBN: 1-4218-1427-7
eBook ISBN: 1-4218-1627-X

Purchase *"The American Child"*
as a traditional bound book at:
www.1stWorldLibrary.org/purchase.asp?ISBN=1-4218-1527-3

1st World Library Literary Society is a nonprofit
organization dedicated to promoting literacy by:

- Creating a free internet library accessible from any
computer worldwide.
- Hosting writing competitions and offering book
publishing scholarships.

Readers interested in supporting literacy
through sponsorship, donations or
membership please contact:
literacy@1stworldlibrary.org
Check us out at: www.1stworldlibrary.ORG
and start downloading free ebooks today.

The American Child
contributed by Tim, Ed & Rodney
in support of
1st World Library Literary Society

To My Father And Mother

PREFACE

The purpose of this preface is that of every preface - to say "thank you" to the persons who have helped in the making of the book.

I would render thanks first of all to the Editors of the "Outlook" for permission to reprint the chapters of the book which appeared as articles in the monthly magazine numbers of their publication.

I return thanks also to Miss Rosamond F. Rothery, Miss Sara Cone Bryant, Miss Agnes F. Perkins, and Mr. Ferris Greenslet. Without the help and encouragement of all of these, the book never would have been written.

Finally, I wish to say an additional word of thanks to my physician, Dr. John E. Stillwell. Had it not been for his consummate skill and untiring care after an accident, which, four years ago, made me a year-long hospital patient, I should never have lived to write anything.

E. McC.

CAMBRIDGE, January, 1913

CONTENTS

INTRODUCTION

One day several years ago, when Mr. Lowes Dickinson's statement that he had found no conversation and - worse still - no conversationalists in America was fresh in our outraged minds, I happened to meet an English woman who had spent approximately the same amount of time in our country as had Mr. Lowes Dickinson. "What has been your experience?" I anxiously asked her. "Is it true that we only 'talk'? Can it really be that we never 'converse'?"

"Dear me, no!" she exclaimed with gratifying fervor. "You are the most delightful conversationalists in the world, on your own subject -"

"Our own subject?" I echoed.

"Certainly," she returned; "your own subject, the national subject, - the child, the American child. It is possible to 'converse' with any American on that subject; every one of you has something to say on it; and every one of you will listen eagerly to what any other person says on it. You modify the opinions of your hearers by what you say; and you actually allow your own opinions to be modified by what you hear said. If that is conversation, without a doubt you have it in America, and have it in as perfect a state as conversation ever was had anywhere. But you have it only on that subject. I wonder why," she went on, half-musingly, before I could make an attempt to persuade her to qualify her rather sweeping assertion. "It may be because you do so much for children, in

America. They are always on your mind; they are hardly ever out of your sight. You are forever either doing something for them, or planning to do something for them. No wonder the child is your one subject of conversation. You do so *very* much for children in America," she repeated.

Few of us will agree with the English woman that the child, the American child, is the only subject upon which we converse. Certainly, though, it is a favorite subject; it may even not inaptly be called our national subject. Whatever our various views concerning this may chance to be, however, it is likely that we are all in entire agreement with regard to the other matter touched upon by the English woman, - the pervasiveness of American children. Is it not true that we keep them continually in mind; that we seldom let them go quite out of sight; that we are always doing, or planning to do, something for them? What is it that we would do? And why is it that we try so unceasingly to do it?

It seems to me that we desire with a great desire to make the boys and girls do; that all of the "*very* much" that we do for them is done in order to teach them just that - to do. It is a large and many-sided and varicolored desire, and to follow its leadings is an arduous labor; but is there one of us who knows a child well who has not this desire, and who does not cheerfully perform that labor? Having decided in so far as we are able what were good to do, we try, not only to do it ourselves, in our grown-up way, but so to train the children that they, too, may do it, in their childish way. The various means that we find most helpful to the end of our own doing we secure for the children, - adapting them, simplifying them, and even re-shaping them, that the boys and girls may use them to the full.

There is, of course, a certain impersonal quality in a great deal of what we, in America, do for children. It is not based so much on friendship for an individual child as on a sense of responsibility for the well-being of all childhood, especially all childhood in our own country. But most of what we do, after all, we do for the boys and girls whom we know and love; and we do it because they are our friends, and we wish them to share in the good things of our lives, - our work and our play. To what amazing lengths we sometimes go in this "doing for" the children of our circles!

One Saturday afternoon, only a few weeks ago, I saw at the annual exhibit of the State Board of Health, a man, one of my neighbors, with his little eight-year old boy. The exhibit consisted of the customary display of charts and photographs, showing the nature of the year's work in relation to the milk supply, the water supply, the housing of the poor, and the prevention of contagious diseases. My neighbor is not a specialist in any one of these matters; his knowledge is merely that of an average good citizen. He went from one subject to the other, studying them. His boy followed close beside him, looking where his father looked, - if with a lesser interest at the charts, with as great an intentness at the photographs. As they made their way about the room given over to the exhibit, they talked, the boy asking questions, the father endeavoring to answer them.

The small boy caught sight of me as I stood before one of the charts relating to the prevention of contagious diseases, and ran across the room to me. "What are *you* looking at?" he said. "That! It shows how many people were vaccinated, doesn't it? Come over here and see the pictures of the calves the doctors get the stuff to vaccinate with from!"

"Isn't this an odd place for a little boy on a Saturday afternoon?" I remarked to my neighbor, a little later, when the boy had roamed to the other side of the room, out of hearing.

"Not at all!" asserted the child's father. "He was inquiring the other day why he had been vaccinated, why all the children at school had been vaccinated. Just before that, he had asked where the water in the tap came from. This is just the place for him right now! It isn't odd at all for him to be here on a Saturday afternoon. It is much odder for *me*" he continued with a smile. "I'd naturally be playing golf! But when children begin to ask questions, one has to do something about answering them; and coming here seemed to be the best way of answering these newest questions of my boy's. I want him to learn about the connection of the state with these things; so he will be ready to do his part in them, when he gets to the 'voting age.'"

"But can he understand, yet?" I ventured.

"More than if he hadn't seen all this, and heard about what it means," my neighbor replied.

It is not unnatural, when a child asks questions so great and so far-reaching as those my neighbor's small boy had put to him, that we should "do something about answering them," - something as vivid as may be within our power. But, even when the queries are of a minor character, we still bestir ourselves until they are adequately answered.

"Mamma," I heard a little girl inquire recently, as she fingered a scrap of pink gingham of which her mother was making "rompers" for the baby of the family, "why are the threads of this cloth pink when you unravel it one way, and white when you unravel it the other?"

The mother was busy; but she laid aside her sewing and explained to the child about the warp and the woof in weaving.

"I don't *quite* see why *that* makes the threads pink one way and white the other," the little girl said, perplexedly, when the explanation was finished.

"When you go to kindergarten, you will," I suggested.

"But I want to know now," the child demurred.

The next day I got for the little girl at a "kindergarten supply" establishment a box of the paper woofs and warps, so well-known to kindergarten pupils. Not more than three or four days elapsed before I took them to the child; but I found that her busy mother had already provided her with some; pink and white, moreover, among other colors; and had taught the little girl how to weave with them.

"She understands, *now*, why the threads of pink gingham are pink one way and white the other!" the mother observed.

"Why did you go to such trouble to teach her?" I asked with some curiosity.

"Well," the mother returned, "she will have to buy gingham some time. She will be a grown-up 'woman who spends' some day; and she will do the spending the better for knowing just what she is buying, - what it is made of, and how it is made!"

It is no new thing for fathers and mothers to think more of the future than of the present in their dealings with their boys and girls. Parents of all times and in all countries have done this. It seems to me, however, that American fathers and mothers of to-day, unlike those of any other era or nation, think, in training their children, of what one might designate as a most minutely detailed future. The mother of whom I have been telling wished to teach her little girl not only how to buy, but how to buy gingham; and the father desired his small boy to learn not alone that his state had a board of health, but that he might hope to become a member of a particular department of it.

We occasionally hear elderly persons exclaim that children of the present day are taught a great many things that did not enter into the education of their grandparents, or even of their parents. But, on investigation, we scarcely find that this is the case. What we discover is that the children of to-day are taught, not new lessons, but the old lessons by a new method. Sewing, for example: little girls no longer make samplers, working on them the letters of the alphabet in "cross-stitch";

they learn to do cross-stitch letters, only they learn not by working the entire alphabet on a square of linen merely available to "learn on," but by working the initials of a mother or an aunt on a "guest towel," which later serves as a Christmas or a birthday gift of the most satisfactory kind! Perhaps one of the best things we do for the little girls of our families is to teach them to take their first stitches to some definite end. Certainly we do it with as conscientious a care as ever watched over the stitches of the little girls of old as they made the faded samplers we cherish so affectionately.

The brothers of these little girls learned carpentry, when they were old enough to handle tools with safety. The boys of to-day also learn it; some of them begin long before they can handle any tools with safety, and when they can handle no tool at all except a hammer. As soon as they wish to drive nails, they are allowed to drive them, and taught to drive them to some purpose. I happened not a great while ago to pass the day at the summer camp of a friend of mine who is the mother of a small boy, aged five. My friend's husband was constructing a rustic bench.

The little boy watched for a time; then, "Daddy, *I* want to put in nails," he said.

"All right," replied his father; "you may. Just wait a minute and I'll let you have the hammer and the nails. Your mother wants some nails in the kitchen to hang the tin things on. If she will show you where she wants them, I'll show you how to put them in."

This was done, with much gayety on the part of us all. When the small boy, tutored by his father, had driven in all the required nails, he lifted a triumphant face to his mother. "There they are!" he exclaimed. "Now let's hang the tin things on them, and see how they look!"

The boy's father did not finish the rustic bench that day. When a neighboring camper, who stopped in to call toward

Elizabeth McCracken

the end of the afternoon, expressed surprise at his apparent dilatoriness, and asked for an explanation, the father simply said, "I did mean to finish it to-day, but I had to do something for my boy instead."

One of the things we grown-ups do for children that has been rather severely criticized is the lavishing upon them of toys, - intricate and costly toys. "What, as a child, I used to *pretend* the toys I had, were, the toys my children have now, *are*!" an acquaintance of mine was saying to me recently. "For instance," she went on, "I had a box with a hole in one end of it; I used to pretend that it was a camera, and pretend to take pictures with it! I cannot imagine my children doing that! They have real cameras and take real pictures."

The camera would seem to be typical of the toys we give to the children of to-day; they can do something with it, - something real.

The dearest treasure of my childhood was a tiny gold locket, shaped, and even engraved, like a watch. Not long ago I was showing it to a little girl who lives in New York. "I used to pretend it *was* a watch," I said; "I used to pretend telling the time by it."

She gazed at it with interested eyes. "It is very nice," she observed politely; "but wouldn't you have liked to have a *real* watch? *I* have one; and I *really* tell the time by it."

"But you cannot pretend with it!" I found myself saying.

"Oh, yes, I can," the little girl exclaimed in surprise; "and I do! I hang it on the cupola of my dolls' house and pretend that it is the clock in the Metropolitan Tower!"

The alarmists warn us that what we do for the children in the direction of costly and complicated toys may, even while helping them do something for themselves, mar their priceless simplicity. Need we fear this? Is it not likely that the "real" watches which we give them that they may "really" tell time, will be used, also, for more than one of the other simple purposes of childhood?

The English woman said that we Americans did so much, so *very* much, for the children of our nation. There have been other foreigners who asserted that we did *too* much. Indubitably, we do a great deal. But, since we do it all that the children may learn to do, and, through doing, to be, can we ever possibly do too much? "It is possible to converse with any American on the American child," the English woman said. Certainly every American has something to say on that subject, because every American is trying to do something for some American child, or group of children, to do much, *very* much.

I

THE CHILD AT HOME

In one of the letters of Alice, Grand Duchess of Hesse, to her mother, Queen Victoria, she writes: "I try to give my children in their home what I had in my childhood's home. As well as I am able, I copy what you did."

There is something essentially British in this point of view. The English mother, whatever her rank, tries to give her children in their home what she had in her childhood's home; as well as she is able, she copies what her mother did. The conditions of her life may be entirely different from those of her mother, her children may be unlike herself in disposition; yet she still holds to tradition in regard to their upbringing; she tries to make their home a reproduction of her mother's home.

The American mother, whatever her station, does the exact opposite - she attempts to bestow upon her children what she did not possess; and she makes an effort to imitate as little as possible what her mother did. She desires her children to have that which she did not have, and for which she longed; or that which she now thinks so much better a possession than anything she did have. Her ambition is to train her children, not after her mother's way, but in accordance with "the most approved modern method." This method is apt, on analysis, to turn out to be merely the reverse side of her mother's procedure.

I have an acquaintance, the mother of a plump, jolly little tomboy of a girl; which child my acquaintance dresses in dainty embroideries and laces, delicately colored ribbons, velvet cloaks, and feathered hats. These garments are not "becoming" to the little girl, and they are a distinct hindrance to her hoydenish activities. They are not what she ought to have, and, moreover, they are not what she wants.

"I wish I had a middy blouse, and some bloomers, and an aviation cap, and a sweater, and a Peter Thompson coat!" I heard her say recently to her mother: "the other children have them."

"Children are never satisfied!" her mother exclaimed to me later, when we were alone. "I spend so much time and money seeing that she has nice clothes; and you hear what she thinks of them!"

"But, for ordinary wear, for play, wouldn't the things she wants be more comfortable?" I ventured. "You dress her so beautifully!" I added.

"Well," said my acquaintance in a gratified tone, "I am glad you think so. *I* had *no* very pretty clothes when I was a child; and I always longed for them. My mother didn't believe in finery for children; and she dressed us very plainly indeed. I want my little girl to look as I used to wish *I* might look!"

"But she doesn't care how she looks -" I began.

"I know," the child's mother sighed. "I can *see* how *her* little girls will be dressed!"

Can we not all see just that? And doubtless the little girls of this beruffled, befurbelowed tomboy - dressed in middy blouses, and bloomers, and aviation caps, and sweaters, and Peter Thompson coats, or their future equivalents - will wish they had garments of a totally different kind; and *she* will be exclaiming, "Children are never satisfied!"

If this principle on the part of mothers in America in providing for their children were confined to such super-ficialities as their clothing, no appreciable harm - or good - would come of it. But such is not the case; it extends to the uttermost parts of the child's home life.

Only the other day I happened to call upon a friend of mine during the hour set aside for her little girl's piano lesson. The child was tearfully and rebelliously playing a "piece." Her teacher, a musician of unusual ability, guided her stumbling fingers with conscientious patience and care. A child of the least musical talent would surely have responded in some measure to such excellent instruction. My friend's little girl did not. When the lesson was finished, she slipped from the piano stool with a sigh of intense relief.

She started to run out of doors; but her mother detained her. "You may go to your room for an hour," she said, gently but gravely, "and stay there all alone. That will help you to remember to try harder tomorrow to have a good music lesson." And the child, more tearful, more rebellious than before, crept away to her room.

"When I was her age I didn't like the work involved in taking music lessons any better than she does," my friend said. "So my mother didn't insist upon my taking them. I have regretted it all my life. I love music; I always loved it - I loved it even when I hated practising and music lessons. I wish my mother had made me keep at it, no matter how much I objected! Well, I shall do it with *my* daughter; she'll thank me for it some day."

I am not so sure that her daughter will. Her music-teacher agrees with me. "The child has no talent whatever," she told me. "It is a waste of time for her to take piano lessons. Her mother now - *she* has a real gift for it! I often wish *she* would take the lessons!"

American mothers are no more prone to give their children

what they themselves did not have than are American fathers. The man who is most eager that his son should have a college education is not the man who has two or three academic degrees, but the man who never went to college at all. The father whose boys are allowed to be irregular in their church attendance is the father who, as a boy, was compelled to go to church, rain or shine, twice on every Sunday.

In the more intimate life of the family the same principle rules. The parents try to give to the children ideals that were not given to them; they attempt to inculcate in the children habits that were not inculcated in themselves.

I know a family in which are three small girls, between whom there is very little difference in age. These children all enjoy coming to take tea with me. For convenience, I should naturally invite them all on the same afternoon.

Both their father and mother, however, have requested me not to do this. "Do ask them one at a time on different days," they said.

"Of course I will," I assented. "But - why?" I could not forbear questioning.

"When I was a child," the mother of the three little girls explained, "I was never allowed to accept an invitation unless my younger sister was invited, too. I was fond of my sister; but I used to long to go somewhere sometime by myself! My husband had the same experience - his brother always had to be invited when he was, or he couldn't go. Our children shall not be so circumscribed!"

There is not much danger for them, certainly, in that direction. Yet I rather think they would enjoy doing more things together. One day, not a great while ago, I chanced to meet all three of them near a tearoom. I asked them - perforce all of them - to go in with me and partake of ice cream. As we sat around the table, the oldest of the three glanced at the other two with a friendly smile. "It is nice - all of us having ice cream with you at the same time," she remarked, and her younger sisters enthusiastically agreed.

To be sure, they are nearer the same age and they are more alike in their tastes than their mother and her sister, or their father and his brother. Perhaps their parents needed to take their pleasures singly; they seem able quite happily to take theirs in company.

I have another friend, who was brought up in a household in which, as she says, "individuality" was the keynote. In her own home the keynote is "the family." She encourages her children to "do things together." Furthermore, she and her husband habitually participate in their children's occupations to a greater degree than any other parents I have ever seen.

Their friends usually entertain these children "as a family"; but not long ago, happening to have only two tickets to a concert, I asked one, and just one, of the little girls of this household to attend it with me. She accepted eagerly. During an intermission she looked up at me and said, confidingly, "It is nice sometimes to do things not 'as a family,' but just as one's self."

Then, for the first time, it occurred to me that she was the "odd one" of her family. All its pleasures, all its interests, were not equally hers. She needed sometimes to do things as herself.

In matters of discipline, too, we find the same theory at work. Parents who were severely punished as children do not punish their children at all; and the most austere of parents are those who, when children, were "spoiled." Almost regardless of the natures of their children, parents deal with them, so far as discipline is concerned, as they themselves were not dealt with.

This implies no lack of love, no lack of respect, for the older generation. On the contrary, it is the sign and symbol of a love, a respect, so great as to permit of divergences of opinion and procedure, in spite of differences of age.

"I am not going to bring up the baby in the way I was brought up, mamma, darling," I once heard a mother of a month-old baby (her first child) say to the baby's grandmother.

"Aren't you, dear?" replied the older lady, with a smile. "Why not?"

"Oh," returned the daughter, "I want her to be better than I am. I think if you'd brought me up conversely from the way you did, I'd have been a much more worth-while person."

She spoke very solemnly, but her mother only laughed, and then fondly kissed her daughter and her granddaughter. "That is what I said to *my* mother when *you* were a month old!" she said whimsically.

Children in American homes, it might be supposed, would be affected by such diversity in the theories of their parents and their grandparents concerning their rearing. They might naturally be expected to "take sides" with the one or the other; or, at any rate, to be puzzled or disturbed by the principle of "contrariwiseness" governing their lives. From their earliest years they are aware of it. The small girl very soon learns that the real reason why she finds a gold bracelet in her Christmas stocking is that mother "always wanted one, but grandma did not approve of jewelry for children." The little boy quickly discovers that his dog sleeps on the foot of his bed mainly because "father's dog was never allowed even to come into the house. Grandpa was a doctor, and thought dogs were not clean."

This knowledge, so soon acquired, would seem to be a menace to family unity; but it is not - even in homes in which the three generations are living together. The children know what their grandparents wished for their parents; they know what their parents wish for them; but, most of all and best of all, they know what they wish for themselves. It is not what their parents had, nor what their parents try to give them; it is "what other children have."

Perhaps all children are conventional; certainly American children are. They wish to have what the other children of their acquaintance have, they wish to do what those other children do. It is not because mother wanted a bracelet, and never had it, that the little girl would have a bracelet; it is because "the other girls have bracelets." Not on account of the rules that forbade father's dog the house is the small boy happy in the nightly companionship of his dog; he takes the dog to bed with him for the reason that "the other boys' dogs sleep with them."

Even unto honors, if they must carry them alone, children in America would rather not be born. A little girl who lives in my neighborhood came home from school in tears one day not long ago. Her father is a celebrated writer. The school-teacher, happening to select one of his stories to read aloud to the class, mentioned the fact that the author of the story was the father of my small friend.

"But why are you crying about it, sweetheart?" her father asked. "Do you think it's such a bad story?"

"Oh, no," the little girl answered; "it is a good enough story. But none of the other children's fathers write stories! Why do *you*, daddy? It's so peculiar!"

It may be that all children, whatever their nationalities, are like this little girl. We, in America, have a fuller opportunity to become intimately acquainted with the minds of children than have the people of any other nation of the earth. For more completely than any other people do American fathers and mothers make friends and companions of their children, asking from them, first, love; then, trust; and, last of all, the deference due them as "elders." Any child may feel as did my small neighbor about a "peculiar" father; only a child who had been his comrade as well as his child would so freely have voiced her feeling.

We all remember the little boy in Stevenson's poem, "My

Treasures," whose dearest treasure, a chisel, was dearest because "very few children possess such a thing."

Had he been an American child, that chisel would not have been a "treasure" at all, unless all of the children possessed such a thing.

Not only do the children of our Nation want what the other children of their circle have when they can use it; they want it even when they cannot use it. I have a little girl friend who, owing to an accident in her infancy, is slightly lame. Fortunately, she is not obliged to depend upon crutches; but she cannot run about, and she walks with a pathetically halting step.

One autumn this child came to her mother and said: "Mamma, I'd like to go to dancing-school."

"But, my dearest, I'm afraid - I don't believe - you could learn to dance - very well," her mother faltered.

"Oh, mamma, *I* couldn't learn to dance *at all*!" the little girl exclaimed, as if surprised that her mother did not fully realize this fact.

"Then, dearest, why do you want to go to dancing-school?" her mother asked gently.

"The other girls in my class at school are all going," the child said.

Her mother was silent; and the little girl came closer and lifted pleading eyes to her face. "*Please* let me go!" she begged. "The others are all going," she repeated.

"I could not bear to refuse her," the mother wrote to me later. "I let her go. I feared that it would only make her feel her lameness the more keenly and be a source of distress to her. But it isn't; she enjoys it. She cannot even try to learn to dance; but she takes pleasure in being present and watching the others, to say nothing of wearing a 'dancing-school dress,' as they do. This morning she said to her father: 'I can't dance, Papa; but I can talk about it. I learn how at dancing-school. Oh, I love dancing-school!'"

Her particular accomplishment maybe of minute value in itself; but is not her content in it a priceless good? If she can continue to enjoy learning only to talk about the pleasures her lameness will not permit her otherwise to share, her dancing-school lessons will have taught her better things than they taught "the other children," who could dance.

That mother was her little girl's confidential friend as well as her mother. The child, quite unreservedly, told her what she wanted and why she wanted it. It was no weak indulgence of a child's whim, but a genuine respect for another person's rights as an individual - even though that individual was merely a little child - that led that mother to allow her daughter to have what she wanted. May not some subtle sense of this have been the basis of the child's happiness in the fulfillment of her desire? She *wanted* to go to dancing-school because the other children were going; but may she not have *liked* going because she felt that her mother understood and sympathized with her desire to go?

A Frenchwoman to whom I once said that American parents treat their children in many ways as though they were their contemporaries remarked, "But does that not make the children old before their time?"

So far from this, it seems, on the contrary, to keep the parents young after their time. It has been truly said that we have in America fewer and fewer grandmothers who are "sweet old ladies," and more and more who are "charming elderly women." We hear less and less about the "older" and the "younger" generations; increasingly we merge two, and even three, generations into one.

Only yesterday, calling upon a new acquaintance, I heard the four-year-old boy of the house, mentioning his father, refer to him as "Henry."

His grandmother smiled, and his mother said, casually: "When you speak *of* father, dear, it would be better to say, 'my father,' so people will be sure to know whom you mean. You may have noticed that grandma always says, 'my son,' and I always say 'my husband,' when *we* speak of him."

"Does he call his father by his Christian name?" I could not resist questioning, when the little boy had left the room.

"Sometimes," replied the child's mother.

"He hears so many persons do it, he can't see why he shouldn't. And there really *is* no reason. Soon enough he will find out that it isn't customary and stop doing it."

This is a far cry from the days when children were taught to address their parents as "honored sir" and "respected madam." But, it seems to me, the parents are as much honored and respected now as then; and - more important still - both they and the children are, if not dearer, yet nearer one another.

In small as well as in large matters they slip into their parents' places - neither encouraged nor discouraged, but simply accepted. Companions and friends, they behave as such, and are treated in a companionable and friendly manner.

The other afternoon I dropped in at tea-time for a glimpse of an old friend.

Her little girl came into the room in the wake of the tea-tray. "Let *me* pour the tea," she said, eagerly.

"Very well," her mother acquiesced. "Be careful not to fill the cups too full, so that they overflow into the saucers; and do not forget that the tea is *hot*" she supplemented.

The little girl had never poured the tea before, but her mother neither watched her nor gave her any further directions. The child devoted herself to her pleasant task. With entire ease and unconsciousness she filled the cups, and made the usual inquiries as to "one lump, or two?" and "cream or lemon?"

"Isn't she rather young to pour the tea?" I suggested, when we were alone.

"I don't see why," my friend said. "There isn't any 'age limit' about pouring tea. She does it for her dolls in the nursery; she might just as well do it for us here. Of course it is hot; but she can be careful."

There are few things in regard to the doing or the saying or the thinking of which American parents apprehend any "age limit." Their children are not "tender juveniles." They do not have a detached life of their own which the parents "share," nor do the parents have a detached life of their own which the children "share." There is the common life of the home, to which all, parents and children, and often grandparents too, contribute, and in which they all "share."

This is the secret of that genuine satisfaction that so many of us grown-ups in America find in the society of children, whether they are members of our own families or are the children of our friends and neighbors.

A short time ago I had occasion to invite to Sunday dinner a little boy friend of mine who is nine years old. Lest he *might* feel his youth in a household which no longer contains any nine-year-olds, I invited to "meet him" two other boys, playmates of his, of about the same age. There chanced also to be present a friend, a professor in a woman's college, into whose daily life very seldom strays a boy, especially one nine years old.

"What interesting things have you been doing lately?" she observed to the boy beside her in the pause which followed our settling of ourselves at the table.

"I have been seeing 'The Blue Bird,'" he at once answered. "Have *you* seen it?" he next asked.

No sooner had she replied than he turned to me. "I suppose, of course, *you've* seen it," he said.

"Not yet," I told him; "but I have read it -"

"Oh, so have I!" exclaimed one of the other boys; "and I've seen it, too. There is one act in the play that isn't in the book - 'The Land of Happiness' it is. My mother says she doesn't think Mr. Maeterlinck could have written it; it is so different from the rest of the play."

Those present, old and young, who had seen "The Blue Bird" debated this possibility at some length.

Then the boy who had introduced it said to me: "I wonder, when you see it, whether *you'll* think Mr. Maeterlinck wrote 'The Land of Happiness' act, or not."

"I haven't seen 'The Blue Bird,'" the third boy remarked, "but I've seen the Coronation pictures." Whereupon we fell to discussing moving-picture shows.

During the progress of that dinner we considered many other subjects, lighting upon them casually; touching upon them lightly; and - most significant of all - discoursing upon them as familiars and equals. None of us who were grown-up "talked down" to the boys, and certainly none of the boys "talked up" to us. Each one of them at home was a "dear partner" of every other member of the family, younger and older, larger and smaller. Inevitably, each one when away from home became quite spontaneously an equal shareholder in whatever was to be possessed at all.

A day or two after the Sunday of that dinner I met one of my

Elizabeth McCracken

boy guests on the street. "I've seen 'The Blue Bird,'" I said to him; "and I'm inclined to think that, if Mr. Maeterlinck did write the act 'The Land of Happiness,' he wrote it long after he had written the rest of the play. I think perhaps that is why it is so different from the other acts."

"Why, I never thought of that!" the boy cried, with absolute unaffectedness. He appeared to consider it for a moment, and then he said: "I'll tell my mother; she'll be interested."

Foreign visitors of distinction not infrequently have accused American children of being "pert," or "lacking in reverence," or "sophisticated." Those of us who are better acquainted with the children of our own Nation cannot concur in any of these accusations. Unhappily, there are children in America, as there are children in every land, who *are* pert, and lacking in reverence, and sophisticated; but they are in the small minority, and they are not the children to whom foreigners refer when they make their sweeping arraignments.

The most gently reared, the most carefully nurtured, of our children are those usually seen by distinguished foreign visitors; for such foreigners are apt to be guests of the families to which these children belong. The spirit of frank *camaraderie* displayed by the children they mistake for "pertness"; the trustful freedom of their attitude toward their elders they interpret as "lack of reverence"; and their eager interest in subjects ostensibly beyond their years they misread as "sophistication."

It must be admitted that American small boys have not the quaint courtliness of French small boys; that American little girls are without the pretty shyness of English little girls. We are compelled to grant that in America between the nursery and the drawing-room there is no great gulf fixed. This condition of things has its real disadvantages and trials; but has it not also its ideal advantages and blessings? Cooeperative living together, in spite of individual differences, is one of these advantages; tender intimacy between persons of varying ages is one of these blessings.

A German woman on her first visit to America said to me, as we talked about children, that, with our National habit of treating them as what we Americans call "chums," she wondered how parents kept any authority over them, and especially maintained any government *of* them, and *for* them, without letting it lapse into a government *by* them.

"I should think that the commandment 'Children, obey your parents' might be in danger of being overlooked or thrust aside," she said, "in a country in which children and parents are 'chums,' as Americans say."

That ancient commandment would seem to be too toweringly large to be overlooked, too firmly embedded in the world to be thrust aside. It is a very Rock of Gibraltar of a commandment.

American parents do not relinquish their authority over their children. As for government - like other wise parents, they aim to help it to develop, as soon as it properly can, from a government of and for their children into a government by them. Self-government is the lesson of lessons they most earnestly desire to teach their children.

Methods of teaching it differ. Indeed, as to methods of teaching their children anything, American fathers and mothers have no fixed standard, no homogeneous ideal. More likely than not they follow in this important matter their custom in matters of lesser import - of employing a method directly opposed to the method of their own parents, and employing it simply because it is directly opposed. This is but too apt to be their interpretation of the phrase "modernity in child nurture." But the children learn the lesson. They learn the other great and fundamental lessons of life, too, and learn them well, from these American fathers and mothers who are so friendly and companionable and sympathetic with them.

Why should they not? There is no antagonism between love

Elizabeth McCracken

and law. Parents are in a position of authority over their children; no risk of the strength of that position is involved in a friendship between parents and children anywhere. It is not remarkable that American parents should retain their authority over their children. What is noteworthy is that their children, less than any other children of the civilized world, rebel against it or chafe under it: they perceive so soon that their parents are governing them only because they are not wise enough to govern themselves; they realize so early that government, by some person or persons, is the estate in common of us all!

One day last summer at the seashore I saw a tiny boy, starting from the bath-house of his family, laboriously drag a rather large piece of driftwood along the beach. Finally he carefully deposited it in the sand at a considerable distance from the bath-house.

"Why did you bring that big piece of wood all the way up here?" I inquired as he passed me.

"My father told me to," the child replied.

"Why?" I found myself asking.

"Because I got it here; and it is against the law of this town to take anything from this beach, except shells. Did you know that? I didn't; my father just 'splained it to me."

American fathers and mothers explain so many things to their children! And American children explain quite as great a number of things to their parents. They can; because they are not only friends, but familiar friends. We have all read Continental autobiographies, of which the chapters under the general title "Early Years" contained records of fears based upon images implanted in the mind and flourishing there - images arising from some childish misapprehension or misinterpretation of some ordinary and perfectly explainable circumstance. "I was afraid to pass a closed closet alone after dark," one of these says. "I had heard of 'skeletons in closets'; I knew there were none in our closets in the daytime, but I couldn't be sure that they did not come to sleep in them at night; and I was too shy to inquire of my parents. What terrors I suffered! I was half-grown before I understood what a 'skeleton in a closet' was."

An American child would have discovered what one was within five minutes after hearing it first mentioned, provided he had the slightest interest in knowing. No American child is too shy to inquire of his parents concerning anything he may wish to know. Shyness is a veil children wear before strangers; in the company of their intimates they lay it aside - and forget it. In the autobiographies of Americans we shall not find many accounts of childish terrors arising from any reserve in the direction of asking questions. In American homes there are no closets whose doors children are afraid to pass, or to open, even after dark.

"American children are all so different!" an Englishman complained to me not long ago; "as different as their several homes. One can make no statement about them that is conclusive."

But can one not? To be sure, they do vary, and their homes vary too; but in one great, significant, fundamental particular they are all alike. In American homes the parents not only love their children, and the children their parents; their "way of loving" is such that one may say of them, "Their souls do bear an equal yoke of love." They and their parents are "chums."

II

THE CHILD AT PLAY

Not long ago I happened to receive in the same mail three books on home games, written by three different American authors, and issued by three separate publishing-houses. In most respects the books were dissimilar; but in one interesting particular they were all alike: the games in them were so designed that, though children alone could play them well, children and grown-ups together could play them better. No one of the several authors suggested that he had any such theory in mind when preparing his book; each one simply took it for granted that his "home games" would be played by the entire household. Would not any of us in America, writing a book of this description, proceed from precisely the same starting-point?

We all recollect the extreme amazement in the Castle of Dorincourt occasioned by the sight of the Earl playing a "home game" with Little Lord Fauntleroy. No American grandfather thus engaged would cause the least ripple of surprise. Little Lord Fauntleroy, we recall, had been born in America, and had lived the whole ten years of his life with Americans. He had acquired the habit, so characteristic of the children of our Nation, of including his elders in his games. Quite naturally, on his first day at the Castle, he said to the Earl, "My new game - wouldn't you like to play it with me, grandfather?" The Earl, we remember, was astonished. He had never been in America!

American grown-ups experience no astonishment when children invite them to participate in their play. We are accustomed to such invitations. To our ready acceptance of them the children are no less used. "Will you play with us?" they ask with engaging confidence. "Of course we will!" we find ourselves cordially responding.

I chanced, not a great while ago, to be ill in a hospital on Christmas Day. Toward the middle of the morning, during the "hours for visitors," I heard a faint knock at my door.

Before I could answer it the door opened, and a little girl, her arms full of toys, softly entered.

"Did you say 'Come in'?" she inquired.

Without waiting for a reply, she carefully deposited her toys on the nurse's cot near her. Then, closing the door, she came and stood beside my bed, and gazed at me in friendly silence.

"Merry Christmas!" I said.

"Oh, Merry Christmas!" she returned, formally, dropping a courtesy.

She was a sturdy, rosy-cheeked child, and, though wearing a fluffy white dress and slippers, she looked as children only look after a walk in a frosty wind. Clearly, she was not a patient.

"Whose little girl are you?" I asked.

"Papa's and mamma's," she said promptly.

"Where are they?" I next interrogated.

"In papa's room - down the hall, around the corner. Papa is sick; only, he's better now, and will be all well soon. And mamma and I came to see him, with what Santa Claus brought us."

"I see," I commented. "And these are the things Santa Claus brought you?" I added, indicating the toys on the cot. "You have come, now, to show them to me?"

Her face fell a bit. "I came to play at them with you," she said. "Your nurse thought maybe you'd like to, for a while. Are you too sick to play?" she continued, anxiously; "or too tired, or too busy?"

How seldom are any of us too sick to play; or too tired, or too busy! "I am not," I assured my small caller. "I should enjoy playing. What shall we begin with?" I supplemented, glancing again toward the toy-bestrewn cot.

"Oh, there are ever so many things!" the little girl said. "But," she went on hesitatingly, "*your* things - perhaps you'd like - might I look at them first?"

Most evident among these things of mine was a small tree, bedizened, after the German fashion, with gilded nuts, fantastically shaped candies, and numerous tiny boxes, gayly tied with tinsel ribbons. "What's in the boxes - presents or jokes?" the little girl questioned. "Have you looked?"

"I hadn't got that far, when you came," I told her; "but I rather *think* - jokes."

"*I'd* want to *know*" she suggested.

When I bade her examine them for me, she said: "Let's play I am Santa Claus and you are a little girl. I'll hand you the boxes, and you open them."

We did this, with much mutual enjoyment. The boxes, to my amusement and her delight, contained miniature pewter dogs and cats and dolls and dishes. "Why," my little companion exclaimed, "they aren't *jokes*; they are *real presents*! They will be *just* right to have when *little* children come to see you!"

When the last of the boxes had been opened and my other less juvenile "things" surveyed, the child turned to her own treasures. "There are the two puzzles," she said, "and there is the big doll that can say 'Papa' and 'Mamma,' and there is the paper doll, with lovely patterns and pieces to make more clothes out of for it, and there is a game papa just *loved*. Perhaps you'd like to play *that* best, too, 'cause you are sick, too?" she said tentatively.

I assented, and the little girl arranged the game on the table beside my bed, and explained its "rules" to me. We played at it most happily until my nurse, coming in, told my new-made friend that she must "say 'Good-bye' now."

My visitor at once collected her toys and prepared to go. At the door she turned. "Good-bye," she said, again dropping her prim courtesy. "I have had a very pleasant time."

"So have I!" I exclaimed.

And I had had. "She was so entertaining," I said to my nurse, "and her game was so interesting!"

"It is not an uncommon game," my nurse remarked, with a smile; "and she is just an ordinary, nice child!"

America is full of ordinary, nice children who beguile their elders into playing with them games that are not uncommon. How much "pleasant time" is thereby spent!

"Where do American children learn to expect grown people to play with them?" an Englishwoman once asked me. "In the kindergarten?"

Undoubtedly they do. In no country except Germany is the kindergarten so integral a part of the national life as it is in America. In our cities, rich and poor alike send their children to kindergartens. Not only in the public and the private schools, but also in the social settlements, and even in the

Sunday-schools, we have kindergarten departments. In the rural schools the teachers train the little "beginners" in accordance with kindergarten principles. Even to places far away from any schools at all the kindergarten penetrates. Only yesterday I saw a book, written by a kindergartner, dedicated to "mothers on the rolling prairie, the far-off rancho, the rocky island, in the lonely light-house, the frontier settlement, the high-perched mining-camp," who, distant indeed from school kindergartens and their equipment, might wish help in making out of what materials they have well-equipped home kindergartens.

"Come, let us play with the children," the apostles of Froebel teach us. And, "Come, let us ask the grown-ups to play with us," they would seem unconsciously to instruct the children.

One autumn a friend of mine, the mother of a three-year-old boy and of a daughter aged sixteen, said to me: "This is my daughter's first term in the high school; she will need my help. My boy is just at the age when it takes all the spare time I have to keep him out of mischief; how shall I manage?"

"Send the boy to kindergarten," I advised. "He is ready to go; and it will be good for him. He will bring some of the 'occupations' home with him; and they will keep him out of mischief for you."

She sent the boy to a little kindergarten in the neighborhood.

About two months later, I said to her, "I suppose the kindergarten has solved the problem of more spare time for your daughter's new demands upon you?"

"Well - in a way," she replied, dubiously. "It gives me the morning free; but -"

"Doesn't the boy bring home any 'occupations'?" I interposed.

My friend laughed. "Yes," she said; "he certainly does! But he doesn't want to 'occupy' himself alone with them; he wants *all* of us to do it with him! We have become quite expert at 'weaving,' and 'folding,' and 'sewing'! But, on the other hand," she went on, "he isn't so much trouble as he was. He wants us to play with him more, but he plays more intelligently. We take real pleasure in joining in his games, and - actually - in letting him share ours."

This little boy, now five years old, came to see me the other day.

"What would you like to do?" I asked, when we had partaken of tea. "Shall we put the jig-saw puzzle together; or should you prefer to have me tell you a story?"

"Tell me a story," he said at once; "and then I'll tell you one. And then *you* tell another - and then *I'll* tell another -" He broke off, to draw a long breath. "It's a game," he continued, after a moment. "We play it in kindergarten."

"Do you enjoy telling stories more than hearing them told?" I inquired, when we had played this game to the extent of three stories on either side.

"No," my little boy friend replied. "I like hearing stories told more than anything. But *that* isn't a game; that's just being-told-stories. The *game* is taking-turns-telling-stories." He enunciated each phrase as though it were a single word.

His mother had spoken truly when she said that her little boy had learned to play intelligently. He had learned, also, to include his elders in his games on equal terms. Small wonder that they took real pleasure in playing with him.

The children cordially welcome us to their games. They ask us to be children with them. As heartily, they would have us bespeak their company in our games; they are willing to try to be grown-up with us.

Elizabeth McCracken

I was visiting a family recently, in which there is but one small child, a boy of eight. One evening we were acting charades. Divided into camps, we chose words in turn, and in turn were chosen to superintend the "acting-out" of the particular word. It happened that the word "Psychical-research," and the turn of the eight-year-old boy to be stage-manager coincided. Every one in his camp laughed, but no one so much as remotely suggested that the word or the stage-manager be changed.

"What does it mean, 'Psychical-research'?" the boy made question.

We laughed still more, but we genuinely tried to make the term comprehensible to the child's mind.

This led to such prolonged and lively argument that the little stage-manager finally observed: "I don't see how it *can* mean *all* that all of you say. Can't we let the whole-word act of it go, and act out the rest? We can, you know - 'Sigh,' 'kick,' 'all'; and 're' (like in music, you know), and 'search!'"

"Oh, no," we demurred; "we must do it properly, or not at all!"

"Well, then," said the boy, in a quaintly resigned tone of voice, "talk to me about it, until I know what it is!"

In spite of hints from the other camp not to overlap the time allotted us, in the face of messages from them to hurry, regardless of their protests against our dilatoriness, we did talk to that little eight-year-old boy about "Psychical-research" until he understood its meaning sufficiently to plan his final act. "If he is playing with us, then he *is* playing with us," his father somewhat cryptically remarked; "and he must know the details of the game."

This playing with grown-ups does not curtail the play in which children engage with their contemporaries. There are games that are distinctly "children's games." We all know of what stuff they are made, for most of us have played them in our time - running-games, jumping-games, shouting-games. By stepping to our windows nearly any afternoon, we may see some of them in process. But we shall not be invited to participate. At best, the children will pause for a moment to ask, "Did you play it this way?"

Very likely we did not. Each generation plays the old games; every generation plays them in a slightly new way. The present generation would seem to play them with a certain self-consciousness; without that *abandon* of an earlier time.

A short while ago I happened to call upon a friend of mine on an afternoon when, her nursemaid being "out," she was alone with her children - a boy of seven and a girl of five. I found them together in the nursery; my friend was sewing, and the children were playing checkers. Apparently, they were entirely engrossed in their game. Immediately after greeting me they returned to it, and continued it with seeming obliviousness of the presence of any one excepting themselves. But when their mother, in the course of a few moments, rose, and said to me: "Let's go down to the library and have tea," both the children instantly stopped playing - though one of them was in the very thick of "taking a king" - and cried, "Oh, don't go; stay with us!"

"My dears," my friend said, "you don't need us; you have your game. Aren't you happy with it?"

"Why, yes," the little girl admitted; "but we want you to see us being happy!"

Only to-day, as I came up my street, a crowd of small children burst upon me from behind a hedge; and, shouting and gesticulating, surrounded me. Their faces were streaked with red, and blue, and yellow lines, applied with crayons; feathers of various domestic kinds ornamented their hats and caps, and they waved in the air broken laths, presumably gifts from a builder at work in the vicinity.

"We are Indians!" they shrieked; "wild Indians! See our war-paint, and feathers, and tomahawks! We hunt the pale face!"

While I sought about for an appropriate answer to make, my little neighbors suddenly became calm.

"Don't we children have fun?" one of them questioned me. "You like to see us having fun, don't you?"

I agreed, and again their war-whoops began. They followed me to my door in a body. Inside I still heard them playing, but with lessened din. Several times during the afternoon, hearing their noise increase, I looked out; each time I saw that the arrival of another grown-up pale face was the occasion of the climactic moment in the game. In order to be wild Indians with perfect happiness the small players demanded an appreciative audience to see them being happy.

Some of us in America are prone to deprecate in the children of our Nation this pleased consciousness of their own enjoyment, this desire for our presence as sympathetic onlookers at those of their games in which we cannot join. We must not allow ourselves to forget that it is a state of mind fostered largely by our National habit of treating children as familiars and equals. Our satisfaction in their pleasures we mention in their hearing. If they are aware that we like to see them "being happy," it is because we have told them, and told them repeatedly. We do not, as in a former time, "spell some of our words" in their company, in order that they may not know all we say. On the contrary, we pronounce all our words with especial clearness, and even define such as are obscure, that the children not only may, but must, fully understand us when we speak "before them." Unquestionably this takes from the play of the children self-forgetfulness of one kind, but sometimes it gives to them self-forgetfulness of another, a rarer kind.

I know a family of children, lovers of games which involve running races. Several years ago one of the boys of this family died. Since his death the other children run no more races.

"We like running races just as much," one of the girls explained to me one evening, as we sat by the fire and talked about her dead brother; "but, you know, *he* always liked them best, because he generally won. He loved to have mother see him winning. He was always getting her to come and watch him do it. And mother liked it, and used to tell other people about it. We don't run races now, because it might remind mother too much."

No matter how joyously American children may play with their elders, or with their contemporaries, whatever enhancement their satisfaction in play with one another may gain from the presence of grown-up spectators, they are not likely to become so dependent upon the one, nor so self-conscious by reason of the other, that they will relinquish - or, worse still, never know - the dear delights of "playing alone." Games played in company may be the finest prose - they are yet prose; games played alone are pure poetry. The children of our Nation are not without that imagination which, on one day or another, impels a child to wander, "lonely as a cloud," along the path of dreamful, solitary play.

How often a child who, to our eyes, appears to be doing nothing whatever, is "playing alone" a delectable game! Probably, only once in a hundred times, and then, by the merest accident, do we discover what that game is.

Among my child friends there is a little boy who takes great pleasure in seeing dramas acted. One spring day I took him to an open-air presentation of "As You Like It."

The comedy was charmingly given in a clearing in a beautiful private park. Orlando had "real" trees and hawthorns and brambles upon which to hang his verses; and he made lavish use of them.

The fancy of my small friend was quite captivated by what he called "playing hide-and-go-seek with poems." "What fun he has, watching her find them and not letting her know he hid

Elizabeth McCracken

them!" he exclaimed.

Later in the season I went to spend a few days at the country home of his parents. Early one morning, from my window, I espied the little boy, stealthily moving about under the trees in the adjacent apple orchard.

At breakfast he remarked to me, casually, "It's nice in the orchard - all apple blossoms."

"Will you go out there with me?" I asked.

"P'aps not to-day," he made reply. "But," he hazarded, "you could go by yourself. It's nice," he repeated; "all apple blossoms. Get close to the trees, and smell them."

It was a pleasant plan for a May morning.

I lost no time in putting it into practice. Involuntarily I sought that corner of the orchard in which I had seen my small friend. Mindful of his counsel, I got close to the apple blossoms and smelled them. As I did so I noticed a crumpled sheet of paper in a crotch of one of the trees. I no sooner saw it than I seized it, and, smoothing it out, read, written in a primary-school hand: -

"The rose is red,
The violet blue,
Sugar is sweet,
And so are you."

Need I say that I had scarcely read this before I entered upon an exhaustive search among the other trees? My amused efforts were well rewarded. Between two flower-laden branches I descried another "poem," in identical handwriting: -

"A birdie with a yellow bill
Hopped upon the window-sill,
Cocked his shining eye and said

'Ain't you 'shamed, you sleepy-head!'"

In a tiny hollow I found still another, by the same hand: -

"'T was brillig, and the slithy toves
   Did gyre and gimble in the wabe;
All mimsy were the borogoves,
   And the mome raths outgrabe."

As I went back to the house, bearing my findings, I met my little boy friend. He tried not to see what I carried.

"I gathered these from the apple trees," I said, holding out the verses. "They are poems."

He made no motion to take the "poems." His eyes danced. But neither then did he say nor since has he said that the verses were his; that he was the Orlando who had caused them to grow upon the trees.

Another child of my acquaintance, a little girl, I discovered in an even sweeter game for "playing alone." She chanced to call upon me one afternoon just as I was taking from its wrappings an *edition de luxe* of "Pippa Passes." Her joy in the exquisite illustrations with which the book was embellished even exceeded mine.

"Is the story in the book as lovely as the pictures?" she queried.

"Yes," I assured her.

Then, at her urgent request, I told her the tale of the "little black-eyed pretty singing Felippa"; of her "single day," and of her singing that "righted all again" on that holiday in Asolo.

The child was silent for a moment after I had finished the story. "Do you like it?" I inquired.

"Um - yes," she mused. "Let me look at the pictures some

more," she asked, with sudden eagerness.

I handed her the book, and she pored over it for a long time. "The houses then were not like the houses now - were they?" she said; "and the people dressed in funny clothes."

The next Saturday, at an early hour, I heard beneath my window a childish voice singing a kindergarten song. I peeped out. There stood my little friend. I was careful to make no sound and to keep well in the shadow. The small girl finished her song, and softly ran away.

"Your little girl serenaded me the other morning," I said to her mother when I saw her a few days afterward. The child had shown so slight an interest in anything in my book except the pictures that I did not yet connect her singing with it.

"You, too!" exclaimed the little girl's mother. "She evidently serenaded the entire neighborhood! All day Saturday, her only holiday, she went around, singing under various windows! I wonder what put the idea into her head."

"Did you ask her?" I questioned, with much curiosity.

"Yes," answered the child's mother; "but she only smiled, and looked embarrassed, so I said nothing further. She seemed to want to keep her secret, the dear baby! So I thought I'd let her!"

And I - I, too, kept it. "Yes, do let her," was all I said.

American children, when "playing alone," impersonate the heroes and heroines of the dramas they see, or the stories they are told, or the books they read (how much more often they must do it than we suspect our memories of our own childish days will teach us), but when they play together, even when they "play at books that they have read," they seldom "pretend." A group of small boys who have just read "Robin Hood" do not say: "Wouldn't it be fun to play that *we* are

Robin Hood and his Merry Men, and that our grove is Sherwood Forest?" They are more apt to say: "It would be good sport for *us* - shooting with bows and arrows. We might get some, and fix up a target somewhere and practise." The circle of little girls who have read "Mary's Meadow" do not propose that they play at being Mary. They decide instead upon doing, in their own proper persons, what Mary did in hers. They can play together, the children of our Nation, but they seem unable to "pretend" together. They are perhaps too self-conscious.

It is a significant circumstance that yearly there are published in America a large number of books for children telling them "how to make" various things. A great part of their play consists in making something - from a sunken garden to an air-ship.

I recently had a letter from a boy in which he said: "The boys here are getting wireless sets. We have to buy part of the things; but we make as many of them as we can."

And how assiduously they attempt to make as many as they can of the other things we grown-ups make! They imitate our play; and, in a spirit of play, they contrive to copy to its last and least detail our work. If we play golf or tennis, they also play these games. Are we painters of pictures or writers of books, they too aspire to paint or to write!

It cannot be denied that we encourage the children in this "endless imitation." We not only have diminutive golf sticks and tennis rackets manufactured for their use as soon as they would play our games; when they show signs of toying with our work, we promptly set about providing them with the proper means to that end.

One of our best-known magazines for children devotes every month a considerable number of its pages to stories and poems and drawings contributed by children. Furthermore, it offers even such rewards as we grown-up writers and painters are offered for "available" products. Moreover, the young contributors are instructed in the intricacies of literary and artistic etiquette. They are taught how to prepare manuscripts and drawings for the editorial eye. The "rules" given these children are identical with the regulations governing well-conducted grown-up writers and artists - excepting that the children are commanded to "state age," and "have the contribution submitted indorsed as wholly original!"

It is a noteworthy fact that hundreds of children in America send in contributions, month after month, year after year, to this magazine. Even more significant is it that they prepare these contributions with all the conscientious care of grown-up writers or painters to whom writing or painting is the chiefest reality of life. So whole-heartedly do the children play at being what their elders are!

An Italian woman once asked me, "The American children - what do they employ as toys?"

I could only reply, "Almost anything; almost everything!"

When we are furthest from seeing the toy possibilities of a thing, they see it. I have among my treasures a libation cup and a *ushabti* figurine - votive offerings from the Temple of Osiris, at Abydos.

A short time ago a little boy friend of mine lighted upon them in their safe retreat. "What are these?" he inquired.

"They came from Egypt -" I began.

"Oh, *really* and *truly*?" he cried. "*Did* they come from the Egypt in the poem -

    "'Where among the desert sands
    Some deserted city stands,
    There I'll come when I'm a man
    With a camel caravan;

And in a corner find the toys
Of the old Egyptian boys'?"

He spent a happy hour playing with the libation cup and the
ushabti - trophies of one of the most remarkable explorations
of our era. I did not tell him what they were. He knew
concerning them all he needed to know - that they could be
"employed as toys." Perhaps the very tiniest of the "old
Egyptian boys" had known only this, too.

"Little girls do not play with dolls in these days!" is a remark
that has been made with great frequency of late years. Those of
us who have many friends among little girls often wonder what
is at the basis of this rumor. There have always been girls who
did not care for dolls. In the old-fashioned story for girls there
was invariably one such. In "Little Women," as we all recall, it
was Jo. No doubt the persons who say that little girls no longer
play with dolls count among their childish acquaintances a
disproportionate number of Jos. Playing with dolls would seem
to be too fundamentally little-girlish ever to fall into
desuetude.

"Girls, as well as boys, play with dogs in these days!" is another
plaintive cry we often hear. But were there ever days when this
was not the case? From that far-off day when Iseult "had
always a little brachet with her that Tristram gave her the first
time that ever she came into Cornwell," to the time when
Dora cuddled Jip, even down to our own day, when the
heroine of "Queed" walks forth with her Behemoth, girls both
in fact and in fiction have played with dogs; played with them
no less than boys. This proclivity on the part of the little girls
of our Nation is not distinctively American, nor especially
childish, nor particularly girl-like; it is merely human.

In few activities do the children of our Nation reveal what we
call the "American sense of humor" so clearly as in their play.
Slight ills, and even serious misfortunes, they instinctively
endeavor to lift and carry with a laugh. It would be difficult to
surpass the gay heroism to which they sometimes attain.

Elizabeth McCracken

Most of us remember the little hunchbacked boy in "Little Men" who, when the children played "menagerie," chose the part of the dromedary. "Because," he explained, "I have a hump on my back!"

Among my acquaintances there is a little girl who is blind. One day I invited her to go picnicking with a party of normal children, one of whom was her elder sister. She was accustomed to the company of children who could see, and she showed a ready disposition to join in the games of the other picnickers. Her sister stayed close beside her and guarded and guided her.

"Let's play blind man's buff," one of the children heedlessly suggested after a long course of "drop-the-handkerchief."

The other children with seeing eyes instantly looked at the child who was sightless, and whispered, "Ssh! You'll hurt her feelings!"

But the little blind girl scrambled eagerly to her feet. "Yes," she said, brightly; "let's play blind man's buff! *I* can be 'It' *all* the time!"

There is a phrase that has been very widely adopted by Americans. Scarcely one of us but uses it - "playing the game." Our highest commendation of a man or a woman has come to be, "He plays the game," or "She plays the game." Another phrase, often upon our lips, is "according to the rules of the game." We Americans talk of the most sacred things of life in the vocabulary of children at play. May not this be because the children of our Nation play so well; so much better than we grown-ups do anything?

III

THE COUNTRY CHILD

One spring, not long ago, a friend of mine, knowing that I had a desire to spend the summer in the "real country," said to me, "Why don't you go to a farm somewhere in New England? Nothing could be more 'really countrified' than that! You would get what you want there."

Her advice rather appealed to my fancy. I at once set about looking for a New England farmhouse in which I might be received as a "summer boarder." Hearing of one that was situated in a particularly healthful and beautiful section of New England, I wrote to the woman who owned and operated it, telling her what I required, and asking her whether or no she could provide me with it. "Above all things," I concluded my letter, "I want quiet."

Her somewhat lengthy reply ended with these words: "The bedroom just over the music-room is the quietest in the house, because no one is in the music-room excepting for a social hour after supper. I can let you have that bedroom."

My friend had said that nothing was so "really countrified" as a New England farm. But a "music-room," a "social hour after supper!" The terms suggested things distinctly urban.

I sent another letter to the woman to whom this amazing farmhouse belonged. "I am afraid I cannot come," I wrote. "I want a simpler place." Then, yielding to my intense curiosity, I added: "Are many of your boarders musical? Is the music-room for their use?"

"No place could be simpler than this," she answered, by return mail. "I don't know whether any of my boarders this year will be musical or not. Some years they have been. The music-room isn't for my boarders, especially; it is for my niece. She is very musical, but she doesn't get much time for practising in the summer."

She went on to say that she hoped I would decide to take the bedroom over the music-room. I did. I had told her that, above all things, I desired quiet; but, after reading her letters, I think I wished, above all things, to see the music-room, and the niece who was musical.

"She will probably be a shy, awkward girl," one of my city neighbors said to me; "and no doubt she will play 'The Maiden's Prayer' on a melodeon which will occupy one corner of the back sitting-room. You will see."

In order to reach the farm it was necessary not only to take a journey on a train, but also to drive three miles over a hilly road. The little station at which I changed from the train to an open two-seated carriage in waiting for me was the usual rural village, with its one main street, its commingled post-office and dry-goods and grocery store, and its small white meeting-house.

The farm, as we approached it, called to mind the pictures of old New England farms with which all of us are familiar. The house itself was over a hundred years old, I afterward learned; and had for that length of time "been in the family" of the woman with whom I had corresponded.

She was on the broad doorstone smiling a welcome when, after an hour's drive, the carriage at last came to a stop. Beside her was her niece, the girl whom I had been so impatient to meet.

She was neither shy nor awkward.

"Are you tired?" she inquired. "What should you like to do? Go to your room or rest downstairs until supper-time? Supper will be ready in about twenty minutes."

"I'd like to see the music-room," I found myself saying.

"Oh," exclaimed the girl, her face brightening, "are you musical? How nice!"

As she spoke she led the way into the music-room. It was indeed a back sitting-room. Its windows opened upon the barnyard; glancing out, I saw eight or ten cows, just home from pasture, pushing their ways to the drinking-trough. I looked around the little room. On the walls were framed photographs of great composers, on the mantelshelf was a metronome, on the centre-table were two collections of classic piano pieces, and in a corner was, - not a melodeon, - but a piano. The maker's name was on it - a name famous in two continents.

"Your aunt told me you were musical," I said to the girl. "I see that the piano is your instrument."

"Yes," she assented. "But I don't play very well. I haven't had many lessons. Only one year with a really good teacher."

"Who was your teacher?" I asked idly. I fully expected her to say, "Some one in the village through which you came."

"Perhaps you know my teacher," she replied; and she mentioned the name of one of the best pianists and piano teachers in New England.

"Most of the time I've studied by myself," she went on; "but one year auntie had me go to town and have good lessons."

At supper this girl waited on the table, and after supper she

Elizabeth McCracken

washed the dishes and made various preparations for the next morning's breakfast. Then she joined her aunt and the boarders, of whom there were nine, on the veranda.

"I should so like to hear you play something on the piano," I said to her.

She at once arose, and, followed by me, went into the music-room, which was just off the veranda. "I only play easy things," she said, as she seated herself at the piano.

Whereupon she played, with considerable skill, one of Schumann's simpler compositions, one of Schubert's, and one of Grieg's. Then, turning around on the piano-stool, she asked me, "Do you like Debussy?"

I thought of what my neighbor had prophesied concerning "The Maiden's Prayer." Debussy! And this girl was a country girl, born and bred on that dairy farm, educated at the little district school of the vicinity; and, moreover, trained to take a responsible part in the work of the farm both in winter and in summer. Her family for generations had been "country people."

It was not surprising that she had made the acquaintance of Debussy's music; nor that she had at her tongue's end all the arguments for and against it. Her music-teacher was, of course, accountable for this. What was remarkable was that she had had the benefit of that particular teacher's instruction; that, country child though she was, she had been given exactly the kind, if not the amount, of musical education that a city child of musical tastes would have been given.

My neighbor had predicted a shy, awkward girl, a melodeon, and "The Maiden's Prayer." One of our favorite fallacies in America is that our country people are "countrified." Nothing could be further from the truth, especially in that most important matter, the up-bringing of their children. Country parents, like city parents, try to get the best for their children.

That "best" is very apt to be identical with what city parents consider best. Circumstances may forbid their giving it to their children as lavishly as do city parents; conditions may force them to alter it in various ways in order to fit it to the needs of boys and girls who live on a farm, and not on a city street; but in some sort they attempt to obtain it, and, having obtained it, to give it to their children.

They are as ambitious for the education of their children as city parents; and to an amazing extent they provide for them a similar academic training. An astonishing proportion of the students in our colleges come from country homes, in which they have learned to desire collegiate experience; from country schools, where they have received the preparation necessary to pass the required college entrance examinations. Surrounded, as we in cities are, by schools especially planned, especially equipped, to make children ready for college, we may well wonder how country children in rural district schools, with their casual schedules and meagre facilities, are ever so prepared. By visiting even a few district schools we may in part discover.

I happened, not a great while ago, to spend an autumn month on a farm in a very sparsely settled section of New Hampshire.

One morning at breakfast, shortly after Labor Day, my landlady said: "School opens next week. The teacher is coming here to board for the winter. I expect her to-day."

"Where does she come from?" I asked.

"From Smith College," the farmer replied, unexpectedly. "This is her second year of teaching our school."

The school-teacher arrived late in the afternoon. My landlady was "expecting" her; so was I, no less eagerly.

"Why were you interested in me?" she inquired, when, on further acquaintance, I confessed this to her.

Elizabeth McCracken

"Because, with a training that fits you for work in a carefully graded school or a college, you chose to teach here. Why did you?"

"For three reasons," she answered. "Country life is better for my health than city life; the people around here are thoroughly awake to the importance of education; and the children - they are such dears! You must see them when school opens."

I did see them then. Also, I saw them before that time. When the news of their teacher's arrival reached them, they came "by two, and threes, and fuller companies" to welcome her. They ranged in age from a boy and a girl of fifteen to two little girls of six. Each and every one was rapturously glad to see the teacher; they all brought her small gifts, and all of them bore messages from their homes, comprising a score of invitations to supper, the loan of a tent for the remainder of the mild weather, and the offer of a "lift" to and from school on stormy days.

The teacher accepted these tributes as a matter of course. She was genuinely glad to see her old pupils. In her turn, she sent messages to their several homes, and gave into the children's hands tokens she had purposely gathered together for them. "We'll meet on Monday at the school-house," she finally said; and the children, instantly responding to the implied suggestion, bade her good-bye, and went running down the dusty road. Each one of them lived at least a mile away; many of them more than two miles.

On Monday I accompanied the teacher to school. The school-house was a small, one-roomed, wooden building. It contained little besides a few rows of desks and benches for the children, two or three maps, and blackboards, a tiny closet filled with worn books, the teacher's desk, and a coal stove. But it had windows on three sides, and was set down in the midst of a grassy meadow bordered with a stone wall.

There were fourteen pupils. They were all assembled in the

school-yard when we arrived. The boys were playing baseball, and the girls, perched on the stone wall, were watching them. The moment they saw the teacher boys and girls alike came to escort her to her place in the school-house. When she was in it, they took their own places - those they had occupied during the former term. There was one "new" pupil, a small boy. He had been so frequently a "visiting scholar" the previous year that his newness was not very patent. There was a desk that he also claimed as his.

"We will sing 'America,'" were the words with which the teacher commenced the new school year, "and then we will go on with our work, beginning where we left off in the spring."

We hear a great deal at the present time concerning the education of the "particular child." In the very best of our private schools in the city each pupil is regarded as a separate and distinct individual, and taught as such. This ideal condition of things prevailed in that little district school in the farming region of New Hampshire. That teacher had fourteen pupils; practically, she had fourteen "grades." Even when it happened that two children were taught the same lesson, each one was taught it individually.

"They are all so different!" the teacher said, when I commented upon the difference of her methods with the various children. "That boy, who hopes to go to college and then teach, needs to get one thing from his history lesson; and that girl, who intends to be a post-office clerk as soon as she finishes school, needs to get something else."

She did not aim to prepare her pupils for college. The district school was only a "grammar school." There was a high school in the nearest village, which was three miles away; she made her pupils ready for entrance into that. In order to attend the high school, more than one child in that neighborhood, year after year, in sunshine and storm, walked two and three miles twice daily. Many a child who lived still farther away was provided by an interested father with a horse and a conveyance with which to make the two journeys a day. No wonder the teacher of that district school felt that the people in the neighborhood were "thoroughly awake to the importance of education"!

As for the children - she had said that they were "such dears!" They were. I remember, in particular, two; a brother and sister. She was eight years old, and he was nine. They were inseparable companions. On bright days they ran to school hand in hand. When it rained, they trudged along the muddy road under one umbrella.

The school-teacher had taught the little girl George Eliot's poem "Brother and Sister." She could repeat it word for word, excepting the line, "I held him wise." She always said that, "I hold him tight." This "piece" the small girl "spoke" on a Friday afternoon. The most winning part of her altogether lovely recitation was the smile with which she glanced at her brother as she announced its title. He returned her smile; when she finished her performance, he led the applause.

Before the end of my visit I became very intimate with that brother and sister. I chanced to be investigating the subject of "juvenile books."

"What books have you?" I inquired of the little girl.

"Ever so many of all kinds," she replied. "Come to our house and look at them," she added cordially.

Their house proved to be the near-by farm. One of the best in that section, it was heated with steam and furnished with running water and plumbing. It had also a local and long-distance telephone. The brother and sister were but two of a family of seven children. Their father, who was a member of the school committee, and their mother, who was a graduate of a city high school, were keenly interested in, and, moreover, very well informed on, the subject of pedagogy. They had read a great number of books relating to it, and were in the habit of following in the newspapers the procedures of the National Education Association's Conventions.

"Your children have a large number of exceedingly good books!" I exclaimed, as I looked at the many volumes on a day appointed for that purpose by the mother of the family. "I wish all children had as fine a collection!"

"Country children *must* have books," she replied, "if they are going to be educated *at all.* City children can *see* things, and learn about them that way. Country children have to read about them if they are to know about them."

The books were of many types - poetry, fiction, historical stories, nature study, and several volumes of the "how to make" variety. All of these were of the best of their several kinds - identical with the books found in the "Children's Room" in any well-selected public library. Some of them had been gifts to the children from "summer boarders," but the majority had been chosen and purchased by their parents.

"We hunt up the names of good books for children in the book review departments of the magazines," the mother said.

When I asked what magazines, she mentioned three. Two she and her husband "took"; the other she borrowed monthly from a neighbor, on an "exchange" basis.

No other children in that region were so abundantly supplied with books; but all whom I met liked to read. Their parents, in most cases unable to give them numerous books, had, in almost every instance, taught them to love reading.

One boy with whom I became friends had a birthday while I was in the neighborhood. I had heard him express a longing to read "The Lays of Ancient Rome," which neither he nor any other child in the vicinity possessed, so I presented him with a copy of it.

"Would you mind if I gave it to the library?" he asked. "Then the other children around could read it, too."

"The library!" I exclaimed.

"Oh, I don't mean the one down in the village," he hastened to explain. "I mean the one here, near us. Haven't you been to it?"

When he found that I had not, he offered to go with me to see it. It turned out to be a "lean-to" in a farmhouse that was in a rather central position with relation to the surrounding farms. The library consisted of about two hundred volumes. The librarian was an elderly woman who lived in the house. One was allowed, she told me, to take out as many books as one wished, and to keep them until one had finished reading them.

"Do you want to take out any?" she inquired.

After examining the four or five shelves that comprised the library, I wanted to take out at least fifty. The books, especially the "juvenile books," were those of a former generation. Foremost among them were the "Rollo Books," "Sandford and Merton," Mary Howitt's "Story-Book," and "The Parents' Assistant."

"Who selected the books?" I asked.

"Nobody exactly *selected* them," the librarian said. "Every one around here gave a few from their collections, so's we could have a near-to library - principally on account of the children. I live most convenient to every one hereabouts; so I had shelves put up in my lean-to for them."

News travels very rapidly indeed in the country. My boy friend told some of the other children that I was reading the *oldest* books in the library. "She takes them out by the armfuls," I overheard him remark.

No doubt he made more comments that I did not overhear; for one morning a small girl called to see me, and, after a few preliminaries, said, "If you are through with 'The Fairchild Family,' may I have it? You like it awfully much, don't you?"

Not only in the secular teaching of their children do thoughtful country parents, in common with careful fathers and mothers living elsewhere, try to obtain the best means and to use them to the best ends; in the religious instruction of their children they make a similar attempt. They are not content to let their children learn entirely at home, to depend solely upon parental guidance. The church, and even the Sunday school, are integral parts in the up-bringing of the most happily situated country children. The little white meeting-houses in the small rural villages are familiar places to the country child - joyously familiar places, at that. The only weekly outing that falls to the lot of the younger children of country parents is the Sunday trip to church and Sunday school.

What do they get from it? Undoubtedly, very much what city children receive from the church and the Sunday school - in quantity and in quality. There is a constant pleasure from the singing; an occasional glimmer of illumination from the sermon; and an unfailing delight from the Bible stories. We can be reasonably sure that *all* children get thus much from the habitual church and Sunday-school attendance. Some, irrespective of city or country environment, glean more.

A small country boy of my acquaintance brought from Sunday school one of the most unique versions of a Scriptural passage with which I have ever met. "Did you go to church this morning?" I inquired of him, one Sunday afternoon, when, catching a glimpse of me under the trees near his home, he came, as he explained, to "pass the time of day" with me.

"Yes," he answered; "and I went to Sunday school, too."

"And what was your lesson about?" I asked.

"Oh, about the roses -"

"Roses?" I interrupted, in surprise.

"Yes," the little boy went on; "the roses - you know - in the gardens."

"I don't remember any Sunday-school lesson about them," I said.

"But there *is* one; we had it to-day. The roses, they made the children have good manners. Then, one day, the children were greedy; and their manners were bad. Don't you know about it?" he added anxiously.

He was but five years old. I told him about Moses; I explained painstakingly just who the Children of Israel were; and I did my best to point out clearly the difference between manna and manners. He listened with seeming understanding; but the next day, coming upon me as I was fastening a "crimson rambler" to its trellis, he inquired solemnly, "Can the roses make children have good manners, *yet?*"

Country children are taught, even as sedulously as city children, the importance of good manners! On the farm, as elsewhere, the small left hand is seized in time by a mother or an aunt with the well-worn words, "Shake hands with the *right* hand, dear." "If you please," as promptly does an elder sister supplement the little child's "Yes," on the occasion of an offer of candy from a grown-up friend. The proportion of small boys who make their bows and of little girls who drop their courtesies is much the same in the country as it is in the city.

In the matter of clothes, too, the country mother, like any other mother in America, wishes her children to be becomingly attired, in full accord with such of the prevailing fashions as seem to her most suitable. In company with the greater portion of American mothers, she devotes considerable time and strength and money to the wardrobes of her boys and girls.

The result is that country children are dressed strikingly like city children. Their "everyday" garments are scarcely distinguishable from the "play clothes" of city children; their "Sunday" clothes are very similar to the "best" habiliments of the boys and girls who do not live in the country.

We have all read, in the books of our grandmothers' childhood, of the children who, on the eve of going to visit their city cousins, were much exercised concerning their wearing apparel. "*Would* the pink frock, with the green sash, be *just* what was being worn to parties in the city?" the little girl of such story-books fearfully wondered. "Will boys of my age be wearing short trousers *still?*" the small boy dubiously queried. Invariably it transpired that pink frocks and green sashes, if in fashion at all, were *never* seen at parties; and that *long* trousers were absolutely essential, from the point of view of custom, for boys of our hero's age. Many woes were attendant upon the discovery that these half-suspected sumptuary laws were certain facts.

No present-day country boy and girl, coming from the average home to the house of city cousins, would need to feel any such qualms. Should they, five minutes' inspection of the garments of those city cousins would relieve their latent questionings. They would see that, to the casual eye, they and their cousins were dressed in the same type of raiment.

How could they fail to be? A large crop of "fashion magazines" flourishes in America. The rural free delivery brings them to the very doors of the farmhouse. By the use of mail orders the mother on the farm can obtain whatever materials the particular "fashion magazine" to which she is a subscriber advises, together with paper patterns from which she can cut anything, from "jumpers" to a "coat for gala occasions."

The approved clothes of all American children in our time are so exceedingly simple in design that any woman who can sew at all can construct them; and, in the main, the materials of which they are made are so inexpensive that even the farmer whose income is moderate in size can afford to supply them. A clergyman who had worked both in city and in country parishes once told me that he attributed the marked increase in ease and grace of manner - and, consequently, in "sociability" - among country people to-day, as compared with country people of his boyhood, very largely to the invention of paper patterns.

"Rural folk dressed in a way peculiar to themselves then," he said; "now they dress like the rest of the world. It is curious," he went on, reflectively, "but human beings, as a whole, seem unable not to be awkward in their behavior if their costumes can possibly be differentiated otherwise than by size!"

It is another queer fact that normal persons would seem to require "best" clothes. They share the spirit of Jess, in "A Window in Thrums." "But you could never wear yours, though ye had ane," said Hendry to her about the "cloak with beads"; "ye would juist hae to lock it awa in the drawers." "Aye," Jess retorted, "but I would aye ken it was there."

I have an acquaintance who is not normal in this matter. She scorns "finery," whether for use or for "locking awa." One summer she and I spent a fortnight together on a Connecticut farm. During the week the farmer and his wife, as well as their two little children, a girl and a boy, wore garments of dark-colored denim very plainly made. The children were barefooted.

"These people have sense," my acquaintance observed to me on the first day of our sojourn; "they dress in harmony with their environment."

I was silent, realizing that, if Sunday were a fine day, she might feel compelled to modify her approbation. On Saturday night the farmer asked if we should care to accompany the family to church the next morning. Both of us accepted the invitation.

Sunday morning, as I had foreseen, when the family assembled to take its places in the "three-seater," the father was in "blacks," with a "boiled" shirt; the mother, a pretty dark-eyed, dark-haired young woman, a pleasant picture in the most every-day of garments, was a charming sight, in a rose-tinted wash silk and a Panama hat trimmed with black velvet. As for the boy and the girl, they were arrayed in spotless white, from their straw hats even to their canvas shoes. The hands of the farmer and his son were uncovered; but the mother and her little daughter wore white lisle gloves. They also carried parasols - the mother's of the shade of her dress, the girl's pale blue. No family in America could possibly have looked more "blithe and bonny" than did that one in "Sunday" clothes, ready for church.

The face of my acquaintance was a study.

In it were mingled surprise and disapproval. Both these elements became more pronounced when we were fairly in the meeting-house. All the men, women, and children there assembled were also in "Sunday" clothes.

My acquaintance has the instinct of the reformer. Hardly were we settled in the "three-seater," preparatory to returning home after the service, when she began. "Do you make your own clothes?" she inquired of the farmer's wife.

"Yes," was the reply; "and the children's, too."

"Isn't there a great deal of work involved in the care of such garments
as you are all wearing to-day?" she further pursued.

"I suppose there is the usual amount," the other woman said, dryly.

"Then, why do you do it - living in the country, as you do?"

"There is no reason why people shouldn't dress nicely, no matter where they happen to live," was the answer. "During

Elizabeth McCracken

the week we can't; but on Sunday we can, and do, and ought - out of respect to the day," she quaintly added.

The city is not a mere name to American country children. Increased train facilities, the improvement in the character of country roads brought about by the advent of the automobile, and the extension of the trolley system have done much to mitigate the isolation of rural communities. The farmer and his wife can avail themselves of the advantages to be found in periodical trips to the nearest city. Like other American parents, they invite their children to share their interests. The boys and girls are included in the jauntings to the city.

I once said to a little girl whom I met on a farm in Massachusetts: "You must come soon and stay with me in the city from Saturday until Monday. We will go to the Art Museum and look at the pictures."

"Oh," she cried, joyously, "I'd *love* to! Every time we go to town, and there is a chance, mother and I go to the Museum; we both like the pictures so much."

This little girl, when she was older, desired to become a kindergartner. There was a training-school in the near-by city. She could not afford to go to and fro on the train, but there was a trolley. The journey on the trolley occupied three hours, but the girl took it twice daily for two years.

"Doesn't it tire you?" I asked her.

"Oh, somewhat," she admitted; "but I was already used to it. We usually traveled to town on it when I was small."

"Countrified" is not the word to apply to American farmers and their families. One might as aptly employ it when describing the people of England who live on their "landed estates." Ignorance and dullness and awkwardness we shall not often find among country children. The boys and girls on the farms are as well informed, as mentally alert, and as attractive as children in any other good homes in America.

We all know Mr. James Whitcomb Riley's poem, "Little Cousin Jasper." The country boy in it, we recall, concluded his reflections upon the happier fortune of the boy from the "city" of Rensselaer with these words:

> "Wishst our town ain't like it is! -
> Wishst it's ist as big as his!
> Wishst 'at *his* folks they'd move *here*,
> An' *we'd* move to Rensselaer!"

Only last summer I repeated this poem to a little girl whose home was a farm not far from a house at which I was stopping.

"But," she said, in a puzzled tone of voice, "no place is as big as the country! Look!" she exclaimed, pointing to the distant horizon; "it's so big it touches the edge of the sky! No city is *that* big, is it?"

IV

THE CHILD IN SCHOOL

An elderly woman was talking to me not long ago about her childhood.

"No, my dear, I did not have a governess," she said, in answer to my questionings. "Neither did I attend the public schools, though I lived in the city. I went to a private school. The pupils in it were the girls of the little social circle to which my parents belonged. There were perhaps twenty of us in all. And there were three teachers; one for the 'first class,' one for the 'second class,' and a French-German-music-and-drawing-teacher-in-one for both classes."

"And what did you study?" I asked.

"Besides French, German, music, and drawing?" my elderly friend mused. "Well, we had the three R's; and history, English and American, and geography, and deportment. I think that was all."

"And you liked it?" I ventured.

"Yes, my dear, I did," replied my friend, "though I used to pretend that I didn't. I sometimes even 'played sick' in order to be allowed to stay home from school. Children then, as now, thought they ought to 'hate to go to school.' I believe most of them did, too. I happened to be a 'smart' child; so I liked school. I suppose 'smart' children still do."

A "smart" child! In my mind's eye I can see my elderly friend as one, sitting at the "head" of her class, on a long, narrow bench, her eyes shining with a pleased consciousness of "knowing" the lesson, her cheeks rosy with expectation of the triumph sure to follow her "saying" of it, her lips parted in an eagerness to begin. Can we not all see her, that "smart" child of two generations ago?

As for her lesson, can we not hear it with our mind's ear? In arithmetic, it was the multiplication table; in English history, the names of the sovereigns and the dates of their reigns; in geography, the capitals of the world; in deportment - ah, in deportment, a finer lesson than any of our schools teach now! These were the lessons. Indeed, my elderly friend has told me as much. "And not easy lessons, either, my dear, nor easily learned, as the lessons of schoolchildren seem to be to-day. We had no kindergartens; the idea that lessons were play had not come in; to us lessons were work, and hard work."

My friend gave a little sigh and shook her head ever so slightly as she concluded. It was plain that she deprecated modern educational methods. "Schools have changed," she added.

And has not the attitude of children toward going to school changed even more? Do many of them "hate to go"? Do any of them at all think they "ought to hate to go"? Is a single one "smart" in the old-time sense of the word?

A winter or two ago I was recovering from an illness in a house which, by great good fortune, chanced to be situated on a suburban street corner, not only near a large public school, but directly on the main route of the children going to and from it. My chief pleasure during that shut-in winter was watching those children. Four times a day - at half-past eight, at half-past twelve, at half-past one, and at half-past three - I would take the window to see them going by. They were of many ages and sizes; from the kindergarten babies to the boys and girls of the ninth grade. None of them could possibly have been described as "creeping like snail unwillingly to school." As a usual thing, they came racing pell-mell down the three streets that converged at my corner; after school they as tumultuously went racing up, homeward. I never needed to consult the clock in order not to miss seeing the children. When I heard from outside distant sounds of laughing and shouting, I knew that a school session had just ended - or was about to begin. Which, I could only tell by noting the time. The same joyous turmoil heralded the one as celebrated the other. Clearly, these children, at least, did not "hate to go to school"!

One of them, a little boy of nine, a friend and near neighbor of mine, liked it so well that enforced absence from it constituted a punishment for a major transgression. "Isn't your boy well?" I inquired of his mother when she came to call one evening. "A playmate of his who was here this afternoon told me that he had not been in school to-day."

"Oh, yes, he is perfectly well!" my friend exclaimed. "But he is being disciplined -"

"Disciplined?" I said. "Has he been so insubordinate as that in school?"

"Not in school," the boy's mother said; "at home." Then, seeing my bewilderment, she elucidated. "When he is *very* naughty at home, I keep him out of school. It punishes him more than anything else, because he loves to go to school."

Another aspect of the subject presented itself to my mind. "I should think he would fall behind in his studies," I commented.

"Oh, no," she replied; "he doesn't. Children don't fall behind in their studies in these days," she added. "They don't get a chance. Every single lesson they miss their teachers require them to 'make up.' When my boy is absent for a day, or even for only half a day, his teacher sees that he 'makes up' the lessons lost before the end of the week. When I was a child, and happened to be absent, no teacher troubled about *my* lost lessons! *I* did all the troubling! I laboriously 'made them up'; the thought of examination days coming along spurred me on."

Those examination days! How amazed, almost amused, our child friends are when we, of whose school-days they were such large and impressive milestones, describe them! A short time ago I was visiting an old schoolmate of mine. "Tell me what school was like when you and mother went," her little girl of ten besought me.

So I told her. I dwelt upon those aspects of it differing most from school as she knows it - the "Scholarship Medal," the "Prize for Bible History," and the other awards, the bestowal of which made "Commencement Morning" of each year a festival unequaled, to the pupils of "our" school, by any university commencement in the land, however many and brilliant the number of its recipients of "honorary degrees." I touched upon the ease with which even the least remarkable pupil in that school could repeat the Declaration of Independence and recount the "causes" of the French Revolution. Finally, I mentioned our examination days - six in January, six more in June.

"What did you do on them?" inquired the little girl.

"Will you listen to that?" demanded her mother. "Ten years old - and she asks what we did on examination days! This is what it means to belong to the rising generation - not to know, at ten, anything about examination days!"

"What *did* you do on them?" the little girl persisted.

"We had examinations," I explained. "All our books were taken away, and we were given paper and pen and ink -"

"And three hours for each examination," my friend broke in. "We had one in the morning and another in the afternoon."

"Yes," I went on. "One morning we would have a grammar examination. Twenty questions would be written on the blackboard by our teacher, and we would write the answers - in three hours. On another morning, or on the afternoon of that same day, we might have an arithmetic examination. There would be twenty questions, and three hours to answer them in, just the same."

"Do you understand, dear?" said the little girl's mother. "Well, well," she went on, turning to me before the child could reply, "how this talk brings examination days back to my remembrance! What excitement there was! And how we worked getting ready for them! I really think it was a matter of pride with us to be so tired after our last examination of the week that we had to go to bed and dine on milk toast and a soft-boiled egg!"

The little girl was looking at us with round eyes.

"Does it all sound very queer?" I asked.

"The going to bed does," she made reply; "and the milk toast and the egg for dinner, and the working hard. The examinations sound something like the tests we have, *They* are questions to write answers to, but we don't think much about them. I don't believe any of the girls or boys go to bed afterwards, or have milk toast and eggs for dinner - on purpose because they have had a test!"

She was manifestly puzzled. "Perhaps it is because we have tests about every two weeks, and not just in January and June," she suggested.

She did not seem disposed to investigate further the subject of her mother's and my school-days. In a few moments she ran off to her play.

When she was quite out of hearing her mother burst into a hearty laugh. "Poor child!" she exclaimed. "She thinks we and our school were very curious. I wonder why," she continued more seriously, "we did take examinations, and lessons, too, so weightily. Children don't in these days. The school-days of the week are so full of holiday spirit for them that, actually, Saturday is not much of gala day. Think of what Saturday was to *us*! What glorious times we had! Why, Saturday was *Saturday*, to us! Do you remember the things we did? You wrote poems and I painted pictures, and we read stories, and 'acted' them. Then, we had our gardens in the spring, and our experiments in cake-baking in the winter. My girls do none of these things on Saturday. The day is not to them what it was to us. I wonder what makes the difference."

I had often wondered; but these reflections of my old schoolmate gave me an inkling of what the main difference is. To us, school had been a place in which we learned lessons from books - books of arithmetic, books of grammar, or other purely academic books. For five days of the week our childish minds were held to our lessons; and our lessons, without exception, dealt with technicalities - parts of speech, laws of mathematics, facts of history, definitions of the terms of geography. Small marvel that Saturday was a gala day to us. It was the one "week day" when we might be unacademic!

But children of the present time have no such need of Saturday. They write poems, and paint pictures, and read stories, and "act" them, and plant gardens, and even bake cake, as regular parts of their school routine. The schools are no longer solely, or even predominantly, academic. As for technicalities, where are they in the schools of to-day? As far in the background as the teachers can keep them. Children do not study grammar now; they are given "language work." It entails none of the memorizing of "rules," "exceptions," and "cautions" that the former study of grammar required. History would seem to be learned without that sometime laying hold of "dates." Geography has ceased to be a matter of the "bounding" of states and the learning of the capitals of the various countries; it has become the "story of the earth." And arithmetic - it is "number work" now, and is all but taught without the multiplication tables. How could Saturday be to the children of to-day what it was to the children of yesterday?

My old schoolmate's little girl had spoken of "tests." In my school-days we called such minor weekly or fortnightly matters as these, "reviews." We regarded them quite as lightly as my small friend looked upon her "tests." Examinations - they were different, indeed. Twice a year we were expected to stretch our short memories until they neatly covered a series of examination papers, each composed of twenty questions, relating to fully sixteen weeks' accumulation of accurate data on the several subjects - fortunately few - we had so academically been studying. It is little wonder that children of the present day are not called upon to "take" such examinations; not only the manner of their teaching, but the great quantity of subjects taught, make "tests" of frequent occurrence the only practicable examinations.

"Children of the present time learn about so many things!" sighed a middle-aged friend of mine after a visit to the school which her small granddaughter attended. "What an array of subjects are brought to their notice, from love of country to domestic science! How do their young minds hold it?"

I am rather inclined to think that their young minds hold it very much as young minds of one, two, or three generations ago held it. After all, what subjects are brought to the notice of present-day children that were not called to the attention of children of former times? The difference would seem to be, not that the children of to-day learn about more things than did the children of yesterday, but that they learn about more things in school. Love of country - were we not all taught that by our fathers as early and as well as the children are taught it to-day by their teachers? And domestic science - did not mothers teach that, not only to their girls, but to their boys also, with a degree of thoroughness not surpassed even by that of the best of modern domestic science teachers? The subjects to be brought to the notice of children appear to be so fixed; the things to be learned by them seem to be so slightly alterable! It is only the place of instruction that has shifted. Such a quantity of things once taught entirely at home are now taught partly at school.

It is the fashion, I know, to deplore this. "How dreadful it is," we hear many a person exclaim, "that things that used to be told a child alone at its mother's knee are now told whole roomfuls of children together in school!"

Certainly it would be "dreadful" should the fact that children are taught anything in school become a reason to parents for ceasing to teach them that same thing at home. So long as this does not happen, ought we not to rejoice that children are given the opportunity of hearing in company from their teachers what they have already heard separately from their fathers and mothers? A boy or a girl who has heard from a father or a mother, in intimate personal talk, of the beauty of truth, the beauty of purity, the beauty of kindness, is fortified in an endeavor to hold fast to these things by hearing a teacher speak of them in a public, impersonal way.

Indeed, is not this unity between the home and the school the great and unique fact in the education of the children of the present time? They are taught at home, as children always have been, and doubtless always will be, an "array of subjects"; and they are taught at school, as children perhaps never before were, other aspects of very nearly all the matters touched upon in that "array." My old schoolmate said that Saturday had lost the glory it wore in her school-days and mine; but it seems to me that what has actually occurred is that the five school-days of the week have taken on the same glory. The joys we had only on Saturday children have now on Monday, Tuesday, Wednesday, Thursday, Friday, *and* Saturday!

It is inevitable, I suppose, that they should handle our old delights with rather a professional grasp. One day recently a little girl, a new acquaintance, came to see me. I brought out various toys, left over from my childhood, for her amusement - a doll, with the trunk that still contained her wardrobe; an autograph album, with "verses" and sketches in it; and a "joining map," such as the brother of Rosamond of the Purple Jar owned.

My small caller occupied herself with these for a flattering length of time, then she said: "You played with these - what else did you play with?"

"I made paper-boats," I replied; "and sailed them. I will show you how," I added.

She watched me with interest while I folded and refolded a sheet of writing-paper until it became a boat.

"There!" I said, handing it to her.

"Have you any more, paper you can spare?" she questioned.

"Of course," I said. "Should you like me to make you more boats?"

"I'll make some things for *you*" she remarked, "if you will let me have the paper."

I offered her the freedom of the writing-paper drawer; and, while I looked on, she folded and refolded with a practiced hand, until the table beside us was covered, not only with boats compared with which mine was as a dory to an ocean liner, but also with a score of other pretty and somewhat intricate paper toys.

"Who taught you to make all these lovely things?" I asked.

"My teacher," answered the small girl. "We all do it, in my room at school, every Friday."

They do so many things! Their grown-up friends are hard put

to it to find anything novel to do with, or for, them. Not long ago a little boy friend of mine was ill with scarlet fever. His "case" was so light that the main problem attached to it was that of providing occupation for the child during the six weeks of quarantine in one room. Remembering the pleasure I had taken as a child in planting seeds on cotton in a glass of water and watching them grow at a rate almost equal to that of Jack's beanstalk, I made a similar "little garden" and sent it to the small boy.

"It was lots of fun, having it," he said, when, quite well, he came to see me. "It grew so fast - faster than the others."

"What others?" I queried.

"At school," he explained. "We have them at school; and they grow fast, but the one you gave me grew faster. Was that because it was in a little glass instead of a big bowl?"

I could not tell him. We had not had them at school in my school-days in a big bowl. They had been out-of-school incidents, cultivated only in little glasses.

They have so many things at school, the children of to-day! If many of these things have been taken from the home, they have only been taken that they may, as it were, be carried back and forth between the home and the school.

I have a friend, the mother of an only child, a boy of eight. Her husband's work requires that the family live in a section of the city largely populated by immigrants. The one school in the vicinity is a large public school. When my friend's little boy reached the "school age," he, perforce, was entered at this school.

"You are an American," his father said to him the day before school opened; "not a foreigner, like almost every child you will find at school. Remember that."

"He doesn't understand what you mean when you talk to him about being an American," the boy's mother said the next morning as we all watched the child run across the street to the school. "How could he, living among foreigners?"

One day, about two months later, the small boy's birthday being near at hand, his father said to him, "If some one were planning to give you something, what should you choose to have it?"

"A flag," the boy said instantly; "an American flag! *Our* flag!"

"Why?" the father asked, almost involuntarily.

"To salute," the child replied. "I've learned how in school - what to say and what to do. Americans do it when they love their country - like you told me to," he added, eagerly. "Our teacher says so. She's taught us all how to salute the flag. I told her I was an American, not a foreigner like the other children. And she said they could be Americans, too, if they wanted to learn how. So they are going to."

The small boy got his flag. The patriotism taught at home and the patriotism taught at school, diverse at other points, met and mingled at that one most fundamental point.

In former days children did not quote their teachers much at home, nor their parents much at school. They do both in these days; occasionally with comic results. A little girl of my acquaintance whose first year at school began less than a month ago has, I observed only yesterday, seemed to learn as her introductory lesson to pronounce the words "either" and "neither" quite unmistakably "[=a]ther" and "n[=a]ther."

"This is an amazing innovation," I said to her mother. "How did she ever happen to think of it?"

"Ask her," said her mother plaintively.

I did inquire of the little girl. "Whom have you heard say '[=a]ther' and 'n[=a]ther'?"

"Nobody," she unexpectedly answered.

"Then how did you learn to say it?"

"Uncle Billy told me to -"

This uncle is an instructor of English in one of our most famous colleges. "My *dear* child," I protested, "you must have misunderstood him!"

"Oh, no," she affirmed earnestly. "You see, papa and mamma say 'eether' and 'neether,' and my school-teacher says 'eyether' and 'nyether.' I told papa and mamma, and they said to say them the way my teacher did; and I told my teacher, and she said to say them the way papa and mamma did! I couldn't say them two ways at once; and I didn't know which one way to say them. So Uncle Billy told me, if *he* were doing it, *he* wouldn't worry about it; *he* would say them '[=a]ther' and 'n[=a]ther'!"

She is a very little girl, only seven; and she has not yet rounded out her first month of school. I suppose before she has been in school a full term she will have discovered the impracticability of her uncle's method of settling the vexed question as to the pronunciation of "either" and "neither." Very likely she will decide to say them "eyether" and "nyether," as her teacher does.

It takes the children so short a time to elevate the teacher to the rank of final arbiter in their intellectual world. So soon, they follow her footsteps in preference to any others along the ways of education. Not only do they pronounce words as she pronounces them; in so far as they are able, they define words as she defines them. In due course, they are a bit fearful of any knowledge obtained otherwise than as she teaches them to obtain it. Is there one of us who has attempted to help a child with "home lessons" who has not been obliged to reckon with this fact? Have we not worked out a problem in "bank discount," for instance, for a perplexed youthful mathematician, only to be told, hesitatingly, "Ye-es, you have got the right answer, but that isn't the way my teacher does bank discount. Don't you know how to do it as she does?" Or, with a young Latin "beginner" in the house, have we not tried to bring order out of chaos with respect to the "Bellum Gallicum" by translating, "All Gaul is divided into three parts," to be at once interrupted by, "Our teacher translates that, 'Gaul is, *as a whole*, divided into three parts.'" If we would assist the children of our immediate circles at all with their "home lessons," we must do it exactly after the manner and method ordained by their teachers.

This condition of things ought not to be displeasing to us, for the reason that, in the main, we have ourselves brought it to pass. The children, during their first days at school, are loyally ready to force the views of their fathers and their mothers, and their uncles and aunts, upon their teachers; and their teachers are tactfully ready to effect a compromise with them. But, before very long, our reiterated, "Your teacher knows; do as she says," has its effect. The teacher becomes the child's touchstone in relation to a considerable number of the "array of subjects" taught in a present-day school. School-teachers in America prepare themselves so carefully for their duties, train themselves to such a high order of skill in their performance, it is but just that those of us who are not teachers should abdicate in their favor.

However, since we are all very apt to be in entire accord with the children's teachers in all really vital matters, our position of second place in the minds of the boys and girls with regard to the ways of doing "bank discount" or translating "*Gallia est omnes divisa in partes tres*" is of small account. At least, we have a fuller knowledge of their own relations with these mathematical and Latinic things than our grandparents had of our parents' lessons. And the children's teachers know more about our relations to the subjects taught than the teachers of our fathers and mothers knew respecting the attitudes of our grandfathers and grandmothers toward the curriculum of that earlier time. For the children of to-day, unlike the children of a former time, talk at home about school and talk at school about home. Almost unconsciously, this effects an increasingly cooperative union between home and school.

"We are learning 'Paul Revere's Ride,' in school," I heard a small girl who lives in Boston say recently to her mother.

"Are you, darling?" the mother replied. "Then, shouldn't you like to go some Saturday and see the church where the lanterns were hung?"

So much did the child think she would like to go that her mother took her the next Saturday.

"You saw the very steeple at which Paul Revere looked that night for the lanterns!" I said, when, somewhat later, I happened to be again at that child's home.

"Twice," she replied. "I told my teacher that mother had taken me, so she took all of us in my room at school on the next Saturday."

Perhaps the most significant influence of the American home upon the American school is to be found in the regular setting apart of an hour of the school-day once, or twice, or even three times a week, as a story hour; and the filling of that hour with the stories, read or told, that in earlier times children never so much as heard mentioned at school by their teachers. It is indeed a pleasant thought that in school-rooms throughout the land boys and girls are hearing about the Argonauts, and the Knights of the Round Table, and the Crusaders; to say nothing of such famous personages in the story world as Cinderella, and the Sleeping Beauty, and Hop-O'-My-Thumb. The home story hour is no less dear because there is a school story hour too.

Elizabeth McCracken

The other afternoon I stopped in during the story hour to visit a room in the school of my neighborhood. The teacher told the story of Pandora and the tale of Theseus and the Minotaur. A small friend of mine is a member of the "grade" which occupies that room. At the end of the session she walked home with me.

"Tell me a story?" she asked, when, sitting cozily by the fire, we were having tea.

"What one should you like?" I inquired. "The story of Clytie, perhaps, or -"

"I'd like to hear the one about Pandora -"

"But you have just heard it at school!" I exclaimed.

"I know," she said; "but I'd like to hear you tell it."

When I had told it, she begged me to tell another. Again I suggested various tales in my repertory. But she refused them all. "Tell about the man, and the dragon, and the ball of string, and the lady -" she began.

And once more when I interposed, reminding her that she had just heard it, she once more said, "Yes; but I'd like to hear it again."

Some of the children whom I have in mind as I write go to private schools and some of them go to public schools. It has not seemed to me that the results obtained by the one type of school are discernibly different from those produced by the other. In the private school there are fewer pupils than in the public school; and they are more nearly alike from the point of view of their parents' material wealth than are the pupils in a public school. They are also "Americans," and not "foreigners," as are so many of the children in city public schools, and even in the public schools of many suburbs and villages. Possibly owing to their smaller numbers, they receive more individual attention than the pupils of the public school; but, so far as my rather extensive and intimate acquaintance with children qualifies me to judge, they learn the same lessons, and learn them with equal thoroughness. We hear a great deal about the differences between public and private schools, and certainly there are differences; but the pupils of the public and the private schools are very much alike. It is considerably easier to distinguish a public from a private school than it is to tell a public- school child from a private-school child.

There are many arraignments of our American schools, whether public or private; and there are many persons who shake their heads over our American school-children. "The schools are mere drilling-places," we hear, "where the children are all put through the same steps." And the children - what do we hear said of them? "They do not work at their lessons as children of one, two, or three generations ago did," is the cry; "school is made so pleasant for them!"

Unquestionably our American schools and our American school-children have their faults. We must try to amend both. Meanwhile, shall we not be grateful that the "steps" through which the children are put are such excellent ones; and shall we not rejoice that school is made so "pleasant" for the boys and girls that, unlike the children of one, two, or three generations ago, they like to go to school?

V

THE CHILD IN THE LIBRARY

One day, not long ago, a neighbor of Colonel Thomas Wentworth Higginson, of honored memory, was talking to me about him. Among the score of charming anecdotes of the dear Colonel that she told me, there was one, the most delightful of all, that related to the time-worn subject of the child in the library. "As a family, we were readers," she said. "The importance of reading had been impressed upon our minds from our earliest youth. All of us liked to read, excepting one sister, younger than I. She cared little for it; and she seldom did it. I was a mere child, but so earnestly had I always been told that children who did not read would grow up ignorant that I worried greatly over my sister who would not read. At last I unburdened my troubled mind to Colonel Higginson. 'She doesn't like to read; she doesn't read,' I confided. 'I am afraid she will grow up ignorant; and then she will be ashamed! And think how we shall feel!' The Colonel considered my words in silence for a time. Then he said: 'There is a large and finely selected library in your house; don't be disturbed regarding your sister, my dear. She will not grow up ignorant. You see, she is exposed to books! She is certain to get something of what is in them!'"

Colonel Higginson's neighbor went on to say that from that day she was no longer haunted by the fear that her sister, because she did not read, would grow up ignorant. Are many of us in that same condition of feeling with respect to the children of our acquaintance, even after we have provided them with as excellent a library as had that other child in which they may be "exposed to books"? On the contrary, so solicitous are we that, having furnished to the best of our knowledge the best books, we do not rest until we are reasonably sure that the children are, not simply getting something from them, but getting it at the right times and in the right ways. And everything and every one conspires to help us. Publishers issue volumes by the dozen with such titles as "The Children's Reading" and "A Guide to Good Reading" and "Golden Books for Children." The librarian of the "children's room" in many a library sets apart a certain hour of each week or each month for the purpose of telling the children stories from the books that we are all agreed the children should read, hoping by this means to inspire the boys and girls to read the particular books for themselves. No effort is regarded as too great if, through it, the children seem likely to acquire the habit of using books; using them for work, and using them for recreation.

Certainly our labors in this direction on behalf of the children are amply rewarded. Not only are American children of the present time fond of reading - most children of other times have been that; they have a quite remarkable skill and ease in the use of books.

A short while ago, spending a spring week-end with a friend who lives in the country, I chanced to see a brilliant scarlet bird which neither my hostess nor I could identify. "It was a redbird, I suppose," I said, in mentioning it later to a city acquaintance.

"What *is* a redbird?" she asked. "Is it a cardinal, or a tanager, or something still different?"

"I don't know," I replied. "Perhaps," I added, turning to her little girl often who was in the room, "*you* know; children learn so much about birds in their 'nature study.'"

Elizabeth McCracken

"No," the child answered; "but," she supplemented confidently, "I can find out."

Several days afterward she came to call. "Do you remember *exactly* the way that red bird you saw in the country looked?" she inquired, almost as soon as we met.

"Just red, I think," I said.

"Not with black wings?" she suggested.

"I hardly think so," I answered.

"P'aps it had a few *white* feathers in its wings?" she hinted.

"I believe not," I said.

"Then," she observed, with an air of finality, "it was a cardinal grosbeak; and the other name for that *is* redbird; so you saw a redbird. The scarlet tanager is red, too, but it has black wings, and it isn't called a redbird; and the crossbill is red, with a few *white* feathers, and *it* isn't called a redbird either. Only the cardinal grosbeak is. That was what you saw," she repeated.

"And who told you all this?" I queried.

"Nobody," the little girl made reply. "I looked it up in the library."

She was only ten. "How did you look it up?" I found myself asking.

"First," she explained, "I picked out the birds on the bird charts that were red. The charts told their names. Then I got out a bird book, and looked till I found where it told about those birds."

"Do you look up many things in the library?" I questioned.

"Oh, yes," the child replied.

"And do you always find them?" I continued.

"Not always by myself," she confessed. "Everything isn't as easy to look up as birds. But when I can't, there is always the librarian, and she helps; and when she is helping, 'most *anything* gets found!"

The public library of my small friend's city, not being the library I habitually used, was only slightly familiar to me. Not long after I had been so earnestly assured that the scarlet bird I had seen was a redbird, I made occasion to go to the library in which the information had been gathered. It was such a public library as may be seen in very nearly every small city in the United States. Built of stone; lighted and heated according to the most approved modern methods; divided into "stack-rooms" and "reading-rooms" and "receiving-rooms" - it was that "typical American library" of which we are, as we should be, so proud. I did not ask to be directed to the "children's room"; I simply followed a group of children who had come into the building with me.

The "children's room," too, was "typical." It was a large, sunny place, furnished with low bookcases, small tables, and chairs. Around two walls, above the shelves, were pictures of famous authors, and celebrated scenes likely to be known to children. At one end of the room the bird charts of which I had so interestingly heard were posted, together with flower charts and animal charts, of which I had not been told. At the other end was the desk of the librarian, who so helped young investigators that, when she helped, *anything* got found.

I seated myself at the little table nearest her desk. She smiled, but she said nothing. Neither did I say anything. The time of day was just after school; the librarian was too much occupied to talk to a stray visitor. I remained for fully an hour; and during that hour a steady stream of children passed in and out of the room. Some of them selected books, and, having obtained them, departed; others stayed to read, and others walked softly about, examining the pictures and charts. All of them, whatever their various reasons for coming to the library, began or ended their visits in conference with the librarian. They spoke just above a whisper, as befitted the place, but I was near enough to hear all that was said.

"We want to give a play at school the last day before Christmas vacation," said one small girl; "is there a good one here?"

The librarian promptly recommended and put into the child's hands a little volume entitled "Fairy Tales a Child Can Read and Act."

A boy, entering rather hurriedly, asked, "Could I have a book that tells how to make a wireless set - and have it quick, so I can begin to-day before dark?"

It was not a moment before the librarian found for him a book called "Wireless Telegraphy for Amateurs and Students."

Another boy, less on pleasure bent, petitioned for a "book about Abraham Lincoln that will tell things to put in a composition on him." And a girl, at whose school no Christmas play was apparently to be given, asked for "a piece of poetry to say at school just before Christmas." For these two, as for all who preceded or followed them, the librarian had help.

"How wonderful, how unique!" exclaimed an Italian friend to whom I related the experiences of that afternoon hour in the "children's room" in the library of that small city.

But it seems to me that the wonderful thing about it is that it is not unique; that in almost any "children's room" in almost any public library in America practically the same condition prevails. Not only are "children's rooms" of a very fine order to be found in great numbers; but children's librarians, as sympathetic and as capable as the librarian of my small friend's library, in as great numbers, are in charge of those rooms. So recognized a profession has theirs come to be that, connected with one of the most prominent libraries in the country, there is a "School for Children's Librarians."

The "children's librarians" do not stop at assisting them in choosing books. The story hour has come to be as important in the "children's rooms" as it is now in the school, as it has always been in the home. Telling stories to children has grown to be an art; there is more than one text-book laying down its "principles and laws." Many a librarian is also an accomplished story-teller, and in an increasing number of libraries there is a story hour in the "children's rooms." Beyond question, we in America have taken every care that our public libraries shall mean something more to the boys and girls than places in which they are merely "exposed to books."

American children read; it is doubtful whether any other children in the world read so much or so intelligently. In our public libraries we plan with such completeness for their reading that they can scarcely escape becoming readers! At home we keep constantly in mind the great importance of inculcating in them a love of books and a wontedness in their use. To so many of their questionings we reply by advising, "Get a book about it from the library." So many of the fundamental lessons of life we first bring to their attention by putting into their hands books treating of those lessons written by experts - written, moreover, expressly for parents to give to their boys and girls to read.

A few days ago I received a letter from a mother saying: "Do you know of a book on hygiene that I can give to my children to read - a book on that subject *for* children?"

Within reach of my hand I had such a book, entitled "The Child's Day," a simply, but scientifically, written little volume, telling children what to do from the hour of rising until the hour of retiring, in order to keep well and strong, able to do good work at school, and to enjoy as good play after school. It was a book that a child not only could read with profit, but would read with pleasure.

At about the same time a father said to me: "Is there any book written for children about good citizenship - a sort of primer of civics, I mean? I require something of that kind for my boy."

A book to meet that particular need, too, was on my book-shelves. "Lessons for Junior Citizens," it is called. In the clearest, and also the most charming, form it tells the boys and girls about the government, national and local, of their country, and teaches them their relation to that government.

It is safe to say that there is practically no subject so mature that it is not now the theme of a book, or a score of books, written especially for children. Every one of the numerous publishing houses in the United States issues yearly as many good volumes of this particular type as are submitted. A century ago a new writer was most likely to win the interest of a publisher by sending him a manuscript subtitled, "A Novel." At the present time a beginner can more quickly awaken the interest of a publisher by submitting a manuscript the title of which contains the words, "For Children."

"Authors' editions" of books we have long had offered us by publishers;"*editions de luxe*" too; and "limited editions of fifty copies, each copy numbered." These are all old in the world of books. What is new, indeed, is the "children's edition." We have it in many shapes, from "Dickens for Children" to "The Children's Longfellow." These volumes find their way into the "children's rooms" of all our public libraries; and, quite as surely, they help to fill the "children's bookcases" in the private libraries to be found in a large proportion of American homes. For no public library can take the place in the lives of the children of a private library made up of their "very own" books. The public library may, however, often have a predo-minant share in determining the selection of those "very own" books. The children wish to possess such books as they have read in the "children's room."

Sometimes a child has still another similar reason for wishing to own a certain book. Only the other day I had a letter from a boy to whom I had sent a copy of "The Story of a Bad Boy." "I am glad to have it," he said. "The library has it, and father has it. I like to have what the library and father have."

Parents buy books for their children in very much the proportions that parents bought them before the land was dotted with public libraries. Indeed, they buy books in larger proportions, for the reason that there are so many more books to be bought! The problem of the modern father or mother is not, as it once was, to discover a volume likely to interest the children; but, from among the countless volumes offered for sale, all certain to interest the children, to choose one, two, or three that seem most excellent where all are so good. A mother of a few generations ago whose small boy was eager to read tales of chivalry simply gave him "Le Morte D'Arthur"; there was no "children's edition" of it, no "Boy's King Arthur," no "Tales of the Round Table." The father whose little girl desired to read for herself the stories of Greece he had told her put into her hands Bulfinch's "Age of Fable"; he could not, as can fathers to-day, give her Kingsley's rendering, or Hawthorne's, or Miss Josephine Preston Peabody's. Like the father of Aurora Leigh, -

> "He wrapt his little daughter in his large
> Man's doublet, careless did it fit or no."

At the present time we do not often see a child wrapped in a large man's doublet of a book; even more seldom do we see a father careless if it fit or no. What we plainly behold is that doublet, cut down, and most painstakingly fitted to the child's little mind.

Unquestionably the children lose something by this. The great books of the world do not lend themselves well to making over. "Tales from Shakespeare" are apt to leave out Shakespeare's genius, and "Stories from Homer" are not Homer. In cutting the doublet to fit, the most precious part of the fabric is in danger of being sacrificed.

But whatever the children lose when they are small, they find again when they come to a larger growth. Most significant of all, when they find it, they recognize it. A little girl who is a friend of mine had read Lambs' "Tales." The book had been given to her when she was eight years old. She is nine now. One day, not long ago, she was lingering before my bookcases, taking out and glancing through various volumes. Suddenly she came running to me, a copy of "As You Like It" in her hand. "This story is in one of my books!" she cried.

"Yes," I said; "your book was written from this book, and some of those other little red books there with it in the bookcase."

The child went back to the bookcase. She took down all the other volumes of Shakespeare, and, sitting on the rug with them, she spent an utterly absorbed hour in turning over their leaves. Finally she scrambled to her feet and set the books back in their places. "I've found which stories in these books are in my book, too," she remarked. "Mine are easier to read," she added; "but yours have lovely talk in them!"

Had she not read Lambs' "Tales" at eight I am not certain she would have ventured into the wide realms of Shakespeare at nine, and tarried there long enough to discover that in those realms there is "lovely talk."

Occasionally, to be sure, the children insist upon books being easy to read, and refuse to find "lovely talk" in them if they are not. It was only a short time ago that I read to a little boy Browning's "Pied Piper of Hamelin." When I had finished there was a silence. "Do you like it?" I inquired.

"Ye-es," replied my small friend; "it's a nice story, but it's nicer in my book than in yours. I'll bring it next time I come, so you can read it."

He did. The story was told in prose. It began, "There was once a town, named Hamelin, and there were so many rats in it that the people did not know what to do." Certainly this is "easier to read" than the forty-two lines which the poem uses to make an identical statement regarding the town named Hamelin. My little friend is only six. I hope that by the time he is twelve he will think the poem is as "nice" as, if not "nicer" than, the story in his book. At least he may be impelled by the memory of his pleasure in his book to turn to my book and compare the two versions of the tale.

The children of to-day, like the children of former days, read because they find in books such stuff as dreams are made of; and, in common with the children of all times, they must needs make dreams. Like the boys and girls of most eras, they desire to make also other, more temporal, things. To aid them in this there are books in quantities and of qualities not even imagined by the children of a few generations ago. The book the title of which begins with the words "How to Make" is perhaps the most distinctive product of the present-day publishing house. No other type of book can so effectively win to a love for reading a child who seems indifferent to books; who, as a boy friend of mine used to say, "would rather hammer in nails than read." The "How to Make" books tell such a boy how to hammer in nails to some purpose. I happened to see recently a volume called "Boys' Make-at-Home Things." With much curiosity I turned its pages, - pages illustrated with pictures of the make-at-home things of the title, - glancing at directions for constructing a weather-vane, a tent, a sled, and a multitude of smaller articles. I thought of my boyfriend. "Do you think he would care to have the book?" I inquired of his mother over the telephone.

"Well, I *wish* he would care to have *any* book!" she replied. "If you want to *try* this one -" She left the sentence unfinished, unless a sigh may be regarded as a conclusion.

I did try the book. "This will tell you how to have fun with your tools," I wrote, when I sent it to the boy.

Except for a laconic note of thanks, I heard nothing from my young friend about the book. One day last week I chanced to see his mother. "What do you think I am doing this after-noon?" she said. "I am getting a *book* for my son, at his own request! He is engrossed in that book you sent him. He is making some of the things described in it. But he wants to make something *not* mentioned in it, and he actually asked me to see if I could find a book that told how!"

"So he likes books better now?" I commented.

"Well - I asked him if he did," said the boy's mother; "and he said he didn't like '*booky*' books any better, but he liked this kind, and always would have, if he'd known about them!"

Whether my boy friend will learn early to love "booky" books is a bit doubtful perhaps; certainly, however, he has found a companion in one kind of book. He has made the discovery quickly, too; for he has had "Boys' Make-at-Home Things" less than a month.

It was an easy matter for that boy's mother to get for her son the particular book he desired. She lives in a city; at least three large public libraries are open to her. As for book-shops, there are more within her reach than she could possibly visit in the course of a week, much less in an afternoon.

The mothers who live in the country cannot so conveniently secure the books their boys and girls may wish or need. I know one woman, the mother of two boys, living in the country, who has to exercise considerable ingenuity to provide her sons with books of the "How to Make" kind. There is no public library within available distance of the farmhouse which is her home, and she and her husband cannot afford to buy many books for their children. The boys, moreover, like so great a variety of books that, in order to please them, it is not necessary to select a book that is not "booky." Their parents are lovers of great literature. "I cannot bring myself to buy a book about how to make an aeroplane, for instance," their mother said to me one day, "when there are so many wonderful books they have not read, and would enjoy reading! Since I must limit my purchase of books, I really think I ought to choose only the *real* books for the boys; and yet they want to make things with their hands, like other boys, and there is no way to teach them how except through books. My husband has no time for it, and there is no one else to show them."

The next summer I went to spend a few days with my friend in the country. The morning after my arrival her boys proposed to take me "over the place." At the lower edge of the garden, to which we presently came, there was a little brook. Across it was a bridge. It was plainly to be seen that this bridge was the work of the boys. "How very nice it is!" I remarked.

"We made it," the older of the boys instantly replied.

"Who showed you how?" I queried, wondering, as I spoke, if my friend had, after all, changed her mind with respect to the selection of books for her children, and chosen one "How to Make" volume.

"It told how in a book," the younger boy said; "a Latin book father studied out of when he was a boy. There was a picture of the bridge; and on the pages in the back of the book the way to make it was all written out in English - father had done it when he was in school. It was a long time before we could *quite* see how to do it; but mother helped, and the picture showed how, and father thought we could do it if we kept at it. And it is really a good bridge - you can walk across on it."

When the boys and I returned to the house my friend greeted me with a merry smile. As soon as we were alone she exclaimed, "I have *so* wanted to write to you about our bridge, patterned on Caesar's! But the boys are so proud of it, they like to 'surprise' people with it - not because it is like a bridge Caesar made, but because it is a bridge they have made themselves!"

Elizabeth McCracken

Another friend of mine, the mother of a little girl, has had a different problem, centring around the necessity of books for children, to solve. She, too, lives in the country, and her little girl is a pupil at the neighboring district school. During a visit in the city home of a cousin the small girl had been a spectator at the city child's "school play," which happened to consist of scenes from "A Midsummer-Night's Dream." When she returned home, she wished to have such an entertainment in her school. "Dearest," her mother said, "we have no books of plays children could act."

"Couldn't we do the one they did at Cousin Rose's school?" was the next query. "Papa says we have *that*."

"I am afraid not," her mother demurred. "Ask your teacher."

The child approached her teacher on the subject. "No," the teacher said decisively. "'A Midsummer-Night's Dream' is too long and too hard. Read it, and you'll see. But," she sagely added, "if you can find anything that is suitable, and can persuade the other children to act in it, I will help you all I can."

That evening, at home, the little girl read "A Midsummer-Night's Dream." "Mamma," she suddenly cried, as she neared the end, "my teacher says this is too long and too hard for us children to do. But we *could* do the play that the people *in it* do - don't you think? It is *very* short, and all the children will like it because it is about poor Pyramus and Thisbe, that we have all read about in school. It isn't *just* the same as the way it was in the story we read; but it is about them - and the wall, and the lion, and everything! Don't you think we could do it? They did the fairy part when I saw it at Cousin Rose's school, and not this at all. But couldn't *we*?"

"I did not like to discourage her," my friend said when she related the tale to me. "*All* the other children were willing and eager to do it, so her teacher couldn't refuse, after what she had said, to help them. I helped with the rehearsals, too, and I doubt if the teacher or I ever laughed so much in all our lives as we did at that time - when there were no children about! The children were so sweet and serious over their play! They acted it as they would have acted a play on the subject of Pyramus and Thisbe written especially for them. *They* weren't funny. No; they were perfectly lovely. What was so irresistibly comic, of course, was the difference between their performance and one's remembrance of regular performances of it - to say nothing of one's thoughts as to what Shakespeare would have said about it. How those children will laugh when they are grown up! They will have something to laugh at that will last them a lifetime. But *poor* Shakespeare!"

I did not echo these final words of my friend. For does not Shakespeare rather particularly like to bless us with the laugh that lasts a lifetime, even if - perhaps especially if - it be at our own expense?

Books are such integral parts of the lives of present-day children, especially in America. Their elders appreciate, as possibly the grown-ups of former times did not quite so fully appreciate, the importance of books in the education of the boys and girls. It may even be that we over-emphasize it a bit. We send the children to the book-shelves for help in work and for assistance in play. In effect, we say to them, "Read, that you may be able to mark, learn, and inwardly digest." It is only natural that the boys and girls should read for a hundred reasons, instead of for the one reason of an older day - the pursuit of happiness in the mere reading itself. "How can you sit idly reading a book when there are so many useful things you might be doing?" was the question often put to the children of yesterday by their elders. To-day we feel that the children can hardly do anything likely to prove more useful than reading a book. Is not this because we have taught them, not only to read, but to read for a diversity of reasons?

American children are so familiarly at home in the world of books, it should not surprise us to find them occasionally taking rather a practical, everyday view of some of the things read. A little girl friend of mine chanced to begin her reading of Shakespeare during a winter when her grown-up relatives were spending a large portion of their leisure going to see stage representations of Shakespeare's plays. She therefore heard considerable conversation about the plays, and about the persons acting the chief roles in them. It happened that "As You Like It" was one of the comedies being acted. The little girl was invited to go to see it. "Who is going to be Orlando?" she inquired; she had listened to so much talk about who "was," or was "going to be," the various persons in the several dramas!

"But," she objected, when she was informed, "I think I've heard you say he is not very tall. Orlando was *such* a tall man!"

"Was he?" I ventured, coming in at that moment. "I don't remember that about him. Who told you he was tall?"

"Why, it is in the book!" she exclaimed.

Every one present besought her to mention where.

"Don't you remember?" she said incredulously. "He says Rosalind is just as high as his heart; that wouldn't be *quite* up to his shoulder. And she says she is *more than common* tall! So he must have been *'specially* tall. Don't you remember?" she asked again, looking perplexedly at our blank faces.

There are so many bonds of understanding between American children of the present time and their grown-up relatives and friends. Is not one of the best of these that which has come out of our national impulse toward giving the boys and girls the books we love, "cut small"; and showing them how to read those books as we read the larger books from which they are made? "What kinds of books do American children read?" foreigners inquire. We are able to reply, "The same kinds that grown-up Americans read." "And why do they read them?" may be the next question. Again we can answer, "For much the same reasons that the grown-ups read them." "How do they use the libraries?" might be the next query. Still we could say, "As grown people use them." And if yet another query, "Why?" be put, we might reply, "Because, unlike any other children in the world, American children are almost as completely 'exposed to books' as are their elders."

Elizabeth McCracken

VI

THE CHILD IN CHURCH

Within the past few months, I have had the privilege of looking over the answers sent by men and women - most of them fathers and mothers - living in many sections of the United States, in response to an examination paper containing among other questions this one: "Should church-going on the part of children be compulsory or voluntary?" In almost every case the answer was, "It should be voluntary." In practically all instances the reason given was, "Worship, like love, is at its best only when it is a free-will offering."

It was not a surprise to read again and again, in longer or in shorter form, such an answer, based upon such a reason. The religious liberty of American children of the present day is perhaps the most salient fact of their lives. Without doubt, the giving to them of this liberty is the most remarkable fact in the lives of their elders. No grown people were ever at any time willingly allowed to exercise such freedom in matters pertaining to religion as are the children of our nation at the present time. Not only is churchgoing not compulsory; religion itself is voluntary.

A short while ago a little girl friend of mine was showing me her birthday gifts. Among them was a Bible. It was a beautiful book, bound in soft crimson leather, the child's name stamped on it in gold.

"And who gave you this?" I asked.

"Father," the little girl replied. "See what he has written in it," she added, when the shining letters on the cover had been duly appreciated.

I turned to the fly-leaf and read this:

"To my daughter on her eighth birthday from her father.

    "'I give you the end of a golden string:
    Only wind it into a ball, -
    It will lead you in at Heaven's gate
    Built in Jerusalem's wall.'"

"Isn't it lovely?" questioned the child, who had stood by, waiting, while I read.

"Yes," I agreed, "very lovely, and very new."

Her mother, who was listening, smiled slowly. "My father gave me a Bible on my birthday, when I was seven" - she began.

"O mother," interrupted her little girl, "what did grandfather write in it?"

"Go and look," her mother said. "You will find it on the table by my bed."

The child eagerly ran out of the room. In a few moments she returned, the Bible of her mother's childhood in her hands. It also was a beautiful book; bound, too, in crimson leather, and with the name of its owner stamped on it in gold. And on the fly-leaf was written, -

"To my daughter, on her seventh birthday, from her father."

Beneath this, however, was inscribed no modern poetry, but

      Elizabeth McCracken

"Remember now thy Creator in the days of thy youth, while the evil days come not, nor the years draw nigh, when thou shalt say, I have no pleasure in them."

The little girl read it aloud. "It sounds as though you wouldn't be happy if you *didn't* remember, mother," she said, dubiously.

"Well, darling," her mother replied, "and so you wouldn't."

The child took her own Bible and read aloud the verse her father had written. "But, mother, this sounds as though you *would* be happy if you *did* remember."

"And so you will, dear," her mother made reply. "It is the same thing," she added.

"Is it?" the little girl exclaimed in some surprise. "It doesn't *seem* quite the same."

The child did not press the question. She left us, to return her mother's Bible to its wonted place. When she came back, she resumed the exhibiting of her birthday gifts where it had been interrupted. But after she had gone out to play I said to her mother, "Are they *quite* the same - the text in your Bible and the lines in hers?"

"It *is* rather a long way from Solomon to William Blake, isn't it?" she exclaimed.

"But I really don't see much difference. The same thing is said, only in the one case it is a command and in the other it is an impelling suggestion."

"Isn't that rather a great deal of difference?" I ventured.

"No, I think not," she said, meditatively. "Of course, I admit," she supplemented, "that the idea of an impelling suggestion appeals to the imagination more than the idea of a command. But that's the *only* difference."

It seems to me that this "only" difference is at the very foundation of the religious training of the children of the present day in our country. We do our best to awaken their imaginations, to put to them suggestions that will impel, to say to them the "same thing" that was said to the children of more austere times about remembering their Creator; but so to say it that they feel, not that they will be unhappy if they do not remember, but that they will be happy if they do. It is the love of God rather than the fear of God that we would have them know.

Is it not, indeed, just because we do so earnestly desire that they should learn this that we leave them so free with regard to what we call their spiritual life? "Read a chapter in your Bible every day, darling," I recently heard a mother say to her little girl on the eve of her first visit away from home without her parents. "In Auntie's house they don't have family prayers, as we do, so you won't hear a chapter read every day as you do at home."

"What chapters shall I read, mamma?" the child asked.

"Any you choose, dear," the mother replied.

"And when in the day?" was the next question. "Morning or night?"

"Just as you like, dearest," the mother answered.

But there is a religious liberty beyond this. To no one in America is it so readily, so sympathetically, given as to a child. We are all familiar with the difficulties which attend a grown person, even in America, whose convictions necessitate a change of religious denomination. Such a situation almost invariably means distress to the family, and to the relinquished church of the person the form of whose faith has altered. In few other matters is so small a measure of liberty under-standingly granted a grown person, even in America. But when a child would turn from one form of belief to another, how differently the circumstance is regarded!

One Sunday, not long ago, visiting an Episcopal Sunday-school, I saw in one of the primary classes a little girl whose parents, as I was aware, were members of the Baptist Church.

"Is she a guest?" I asked her teacher.

"Oh, no," she replied; "she is a regular member of the Sunday-school; she comes every Sunday. She was christened at Easter; I am her godmother."

"But don't her father and mother belong to the Baptist Church?" I questioned.

"Yes," said the child's Sunday-school teacher. "But she came to church one Sunday with some new playmates of hers, whose parents are Episcopalians, to see a baby christened. Then her little friends told her how they had all been christened, as babies; and when she found that she hadn't been, she wanted to be. So her father and mother let her, and she comes to Sunday-school here."

"Where does she go to church?" I found myself inquiring.

"To the Baptist Church, with her father and mother," was the reply. "She asked them to let her come to Sunday-school here; but it never occurred to her to think of going to church excepting with them."

Somewhat later I chanced to meet the child's mother. It was not long before she spoke to me concerning her little girl's membership in the Episcopal Sunday-school. "What were her father and I to do?" the mother said. "We didn't feel justified in standing in her way. She wanted to be christened; it seemed to mean something real to her -" she broke off. "What *were* we to do?" she repeated. "It would be a dreadful thing to check a child's aspiration toward God! Of course she is only a little girl, and she wanted to be like the others. Her father and I thought of that, naturally. But -" Again she stopped. "One can never tell," she went on, "what is in the mind of a child, nor what may be happening to its spirit. Samuel was a very little child when God spoke to him," she concluded, simply.

Quite as far as that mother, has another mother of my acquaintance let her little girl go along the way of religious freedom. One day I went with her and the child to an Italian jewelry shop. Among the things there was a rosary of coral and silver. The little girl, attracted by its glitter and color, seized it and slipped it over her head. "Look, mother," she said, "see this lovely necklace!"

Her mother gently took it from her. "It isn't a necklace," she explained; "it is called a rosary. You mustn't play with it; because it is something some people use to say their prayers with."

The child's mother is of Scotch birth and New England upbringing. The little girl has been accustomed to a form of religion and to an attitude toward the things of religion that are beautiful, but austerely beautiful. She is an imaginative child; and she caught eagerly at the poetical element thus, for the first time, associated with prayer. "Tell me how!" she begged.

When next I was in the little girl's bedroom, I saw the coral and silver rosary hanging on one of the head-posts of her bed. "Yes, my dear," her mother explained to me, "I got the rosary for her. She wanted it - 'to say my prayers with,' she said; so I got it. After all, the important thing is that she says her prayers."

Among my treasures I have a rosary, brought to me from the Holy Land. I have had it for a long time, and it has hung on the frame of a photograph of Bellini's lovely Madonna. This little girl has always liked that picture, and she has often spoken to me about it. But she had never mentioned the rosary, which not only is made of dark wood, but is darker still with its centuries of age. One day after the rosary of pink coral and bright silver had been given her she came to see me. Passing through the room where the Madonna is, she stopped to look at it. At once she exclaimed, "*You* have a rosary!"

"Yes," I said; "it came from the Holy Land." I took it down, and put it into her hands. "It has been in Bethlehem," I went on, "and in Jerusalem. It is very old; it belonged to a saint - like St. Francis, who was such friends with the birds, you remember."

"I suppose the saint used it to say his prayers with?" the little girl observed. Then, the question evidently occurring to her for the first time, she asked, eagerly, "What prayers did he say, do you think?"

When I had in some part replied, I said, this question indeed occurring to me for the first time, "What prayers do you say?"

"Oh," she replied, instantly, "I say, 'Our Father,' and 'Now I lay me,' and 'God bless' all the different ones at home, and in other places, that I know. I say all that; and it takes all the beads. So I say, 'The Lord is my Shepherd' last, for the cross." She was silent for a moment, but I said nothing, and she went on. "I know 'In my Father's house are many mansions,' and 'Though I speak with the tongues of men and angels.' I might say them sometimes instead, mightn't I?"

I told this to one of my friends who is a devout Roman Catholic. "It shows," she said, "what the rosary can do for religion!"

But it seemed to me that it showed rather what religion could do for the rosary. Had the child's mother, Scotch by birth, New England by breeding, not been a truly religious woman she would not have bade her little girl handle with reverence the emblem of a faith so unlike her own; she would not have said, "Don't play with it." As for the small girl, had she never learned to "say prayers," she would not have desired the rosary to say them "with." And it was not the silver cross hanging on her rosary that influenced her to "say last," for it, the best psalm and "spiritual song" she knew; it was the understanding she had been given by careful teaching of the meaning of that symbol. Above all, had the little girl, after being taught to pray, not been left free to pray as her childish heart inclined, that rosary would scarcely have found a place on the head-post of her small bed.

It may be for the very reason that the children are not compelled to think and to feel in the things of religion as their parents do that fathers and mothers in America so frankly tell their boys and girls exactly what they do think and just how they do feel. The children may not ever understand the religious experiences through which their parents are passing, but they often know what those experiences are. Moreover, they sometimes partake of them.

Among my child friends there is a little girl, an only child, whose father died not a great while ago. The little girl had always had a share in the joys of her parents. It surprised no one who knew the family that the mother in her grief turned to the child for comfort; and that together they bore their great bereavement. Indeed, so completely did this occur that the little girl for a time hardly saw any one excepting her mother and her governess. After a suitable interval, an old friend of the family approached the mother on the subject. "Your little girl is only eight years old," she said, gently. "Oughtn't she perhaps to go to see her playmates, and have them come to see her, again, now?"

The mother saw the wisdom of the suggestion. The child continued to spend much of her time with her mother, but she gradually resumed her former childish occupations. She had always been a gregarious little girl; once more her nursery was a merry, even an hilarious, place.

One Saturday a short time ago she was among the six small guests invited to the birthday luncheon of another little girl friend of mine. Along with several other grown-ups I had been invited to come and lend a hand at this festivity. I arrived just as the children were going into the dining-room, where the table set forth for their especial use, and bright with the light of the seven candles on the cake, safely placed in the centre, awaited them. They climbed into their chairs, and then all seven of them paused. "Mother," said the little girl of the house, "who shall say grace?"

"*I* can!"

"Let *me*!"

"I *always* do at home!"

These and other exclamations were made before the mother could reply. When she was able to get a hearing, she suggested, "I think each one of you might, since you all can and would like to."

"You say it first," said one of the children to her little hostess, "because it is your birthday."

At a nod from her mother, the little girl said the Selkirk grace:-

>"Some hae meat and canna eat,
>And some wad eat that want it;
>But we hae meat and we can eat,
>And sae the Lord be thankit."

Then another small girl said her grace, which was Herrick's: -

>"Here a little child I stand,
>Heaving up my either hand;
>Cold as paddocks though they be,
>Here I lift them up to Thee,
>For a benison to fall
>On our meat and on us all
>Amen."

The next little girl said Stevenson's: -

> "It is very nice to think
> The world is full of meat and drink,
> And little children saying grace
> In every Christian kind of place."

The succeeding little guests said the dear and familiar "blessing" of so many children: -

"For what we are about to receive, O Lord, make us truly thankful."

My little friend into whose life so grievous a sorrow had come was the last to say her grace. It was the poem of Miss Josephine Preston Peabody entitled "Before Meat: -

> "Hunger of the world.
> When we ask a grace
> Be remembered here with us,
> By the vacant place.
>
> "Thirst with nought to drink,
> Sorrow more than mine,
> May God some day make you laugh,
> With water turned to wine!"

There was a silence when she finished, among the children as well as among the grown persons present. "I don't *quite* understand what your grace means," the little girl of the house said at last to her small guest.

"It means that I still have my mamma, and she still has me," replied the child. "Some people haven't anybody. It means that; and it means we ask God to let them have Him. My mamma told me, when she taught it to me to say instead of the grace I used to say when we had my papa."

The little girl explained with the simple seriousness and

sweetness so characteristic of the answers children make to questions asked them regarding things in any degree mystical. The other small girls listened as sweetly and as seriously. Then, with one accord, they returned to the gay delights of the occasion. They were a laughing, prattling, eagerly happy little party, and of them all not one was more blithe than the little girl who had said grace last.

The child's intimate companionship with her mother in the sorrow which was her sorrow too had not taken from her the ability for participation in childish happiness, also hers by right. Was not this because the companionship was of so deep a nature? The mother, in letting her little girl share her grief, let her share too the knowledge of the source to which she looked for consolation. Above all, she not only told her of heavier sorrows; she told her how those greater griefs might be lightened. Children in America enter into so many of the things of their parents' lives, is it not good that they are given their parts even in those spiritual things that are most near and sacred?

I have among my friends a little boy whose father finds God most surely in the operation of natural law. Indeed, he has often both shocked and distressed certain of his neighbors by declaring it to be his belief that nowhere else could God be found. "His poor wife!" they were wont to exclaim; "what must she think of such opinions?" And later, when the little boy was born, "That unfortunate baby!" they sighed; "how will his mother teach him religion when his father has these strange ideas?" That the wife seemed untroubled by the views of her husband, and that the baby, as he grew into little-boyhood, appeared very similar to other children as far as prayers and Bible stories and even attendance at church were concerned, did not reassure the disturbed neighbors. For the child's father continued to express - if possible, more decidedly - his disquieting convictions. "Evidently, though," said one neighbor, "he doesn't put such thoughts into the head of his child."

Apparently he did not. I knew the small boy rather intimately, and I was aware that his father, after the custom of most American parents, took the child into his confidence with regard to many other matters. The little boy was well acquainted with his father's political belief, for example. I had had early evidence of this. But it was not until a much later time, and then indirectly, that I saw that the little boy was possessed too of a knowledge of his father's religious faith.

I was ill in a hospital a year or two ago, and the little boy came with his mother to see me. A clergyman happened to call at the same time. It was Sunday, and the clergyman suggested to my small friend that he say a psalm or a hymn for me.

"My new one, that daddy has just taught me?" the child inquired, turning to his mother.

She smiled at him. "Yes, dearest," she said gently.

The little boy came and stood beside my bed, and, in a voice that betokened a love and understanding of every line, repeated Mrs. Browning's lovely poem: -

"They say that God lives very high!
But if you look above the pines,
You cannot see our God. And why?

"And if you dig down in the mines,
You never see Him in the gold,
Though from Him all that's glory shines.

"God is so good, He wears a fold
Of heaven and earth across His face -
Like secrets kept, for love, untold.

"But still I feel that His embrace
Slides down, by thrills, through all things made,
Through sight and sound of every place:

Elizabeth McCracken

"As if my tender mother laid
On my shut lids, her kisses' pressure,
Half-waking me at night; and said,
'Who kissed you through the dark, dear guesser?'"

Beyond question the clergyman had expected a less unusual selection than this; but he smiled very kindly at the little boy as he said the beautiful words. At the conclusion he merely said, "You have a good father, my boy."

"Do you like my new hymn?" the child asked me.

"Yes," I replied. "Did your father tell you what it means?" I added, suddenly curious.

"No," said my small friend; "I didn't ask him. You see," he supplemented, "it tells *itself* what it means!"

The things of religion so often to the children tell themselves what they mean! Only the other day I heard a little girl recounting to her young uncle, learned in the higher criticism, the story of the Creation.

"Just only *six days* it took God to make *everything*" she said; "think of that!"

"My dear child," remonstrated her uncle, "*that* isn't the point at all - the *amount* of time it required! As a matter of fact, it took thousands of years to make the world. The word 'day' in that connection means a certain period of time, not twenty-four hours."

"Oh!" cried the little girl, in disappointment; "that takes the wonderfulness out of it!"

"Not at all," protested her young uncle. "And, supposing it did, can you not see that the world could not have been made in six of *our* days?"

"Why," said the child, in surprise, "I should think it could have been!"

"For what reason?" her uncle asked, in equal amazement.

"Because God was doing it!" the child exclaimed.

Her uncle did not at once reply. When he did, it was to say, "You are right about *that*, my dear."

Sometimes it happens that a child finds in our careful explanation of the meaning of a religious belief or practice a different or a further significance than we have indicated. I once had an especially striking experience of this kind.

I was visiting a family in which there were several children, cared for by a nurse of the old-fashioned, old-world type. She was a woman well beyond middle age, and of a frank and simple piety. There was hardly a circumstance of daily life for which she was not ready with an accustomed ejaculatory prayer or thanksgiving. One day I chanced to speak to her of a mutual friend, long dead. "God rest her soul!" said the old nurse, in a low tone.

"Why did she say that?" the little four-year-old girl of the house asked me. "I never heard her say that before!"

"It is a prayer that some persons always say when speaking of any one who is dead; especially any one they knew and loved," I explained.

Later in the day, turning over a portfolio of photographs with the little girl, I took up a picture of a fine, faithful-eyed dog. "Whose dog is this?" I asked. "What a good one he is!"

"He was ours," replied the child, "and he was very good; we liked him. But he is dead now -" She paused as if struck by a sudden remembrance. Then, "God rest his soul!" she sighed, softly.

Most of the answers I read in response to the question, "Should churchgoing on the part of children be compulsory or voluntary?" did not end with the brief statement that it should be voluntary, and the reason why; a considerable number of them went on to say: "The children should of course be inspired and encouraged to go. They should be taught that it is a privilege. Their Sunday-school teachers and their minister, as well as their parents, can help to make them wish to go."

Certainly their Sunday-school teachers and ministers can, and do. The answers I have quoted took for granted the attendance of children at Sunday-school. Not one of them suggested that this was a matter admitting of free choice on the part of the children. "But it isn't," declared an experienced Sunday-school teacher who is a friend of mine when I said this to her. "Going to Sunday-school isn't worship; it is learning whom to worship and how. Naturally, children go, just as they go to week-day school, whether they like to or not; I must grant," she added by way of amendment, "that they usually do like to go!"

Our Sunday-schools have become more and more like our week-day schools. The boys and girls are taught in them whom to worship and how, but they are taught very much after the manner that, in the week-day schools, they are instructed concerning secular things. That custom, belonging to a time not so far in the past but that many of us remember it, of consigning the "infant class" of the Sunday-school to any amiable young girl in the parish who could promise to be reasonably regular in meeting it does not obtain at the present day. Sunday-school teachers are trained, and trained with increasing care and thoroughness, for their task.

Readiness to teach is no longer a sufficient credential. The amiable young girl must now not only be willing to teach, she must also be willing to learn how to teach. In the earlier time practically any well-disposed young man of the congregation who would consent to take charge of a class of boys was eagerly allotted that class without further parley. This, too, is not now the case. The young man, before beginning to teach the boys, is obliged to prepare himself somewhat specifically for such work. In my own parish the boys' classes of the Sunday-school are taught by young men who are students in the Theological School of which my parish church is the chapel. In an adjacent parish the "infant class" is in charge of an accomplished kindergartner. Surely such persons are well qualified to help to inspire and to encourage the children to regard churchgoing as a privilege, and to make them wish to go!

And the minister! I am inclined to think that the minister helps more than any one else, except the father and mother, to give the children this inspiration, this encouragement. Children go to church now, when churchgoing is voluntary, quite as much as they went when it was compulsory. They learn very early to wish to go; they see with small difficulty that it is a privilege. Their Sunday-school teachers might help them, even their parents might help them, but, unless the minister helped them, would this be so?

There are so many ways in which the minister does his part in this matter of the child's relation to the church, and to those things for which the church stands. They are happily familiar to us through our child friends: the "children's service" at Christmas and at Easter; the "talks to children" on certain Sundays of the year. These are some of them. And there are other, more individual, more intimate ways.

The other day a little girl who is a friend of mine asked me to make out a list of books likely to be found in the "children's room" of the near-by public library that I thought she would enjoy reading. On the list I put "The Little Lame Prince," the charming story by Dinah Mulock. Having completed the list, I read it aloud to the little girl. When I reached Miss Mulock's book, she interrupted me.

"'The Little Lame Prince,' did you say? Is that in the library? I thought it was in the Bible."

"The Bible!" I exclaimed.

"Yes," the child said, in some surprise; "don't you remember? He was Jonathan's little boy - Jonathan, that was David's friend - David, that killed the giant, you know."

I at once investigated. The little girl was quite correct. "Who told you about him?" I inquired.

"Our minister," she replied. "He read it to me and some of the other children."

This, too, a bit later, I investigated. I found that the minister had not read the story as it is written in the Bible, but a version of it written by himself especially for this purpose and entitled "The Little Lame Prince."

At church, as elsewhere, the children of our nation are quick to observe, and to make their own, opportunities for doing as the grown-ups do. When occasion arises, they slip with cheerful and confiding ease into the places of their elders.

One Sunday, last summer, I chanced to attend a church in a little seaside village. When the moment arrived for taking up the collection, no one went forward to attend to that duty. I was told afterward that the man who always did it was most unprecedentedly absent. There were a number of other men in the rather large congregation, but none of them stirred as the clergyman stood waiting after having read several offertory sentences. I understood afterward that they "felt bashful," not being used to taking up the collection. The clergyman hesitated for a moment, and then read another offertory sentence. As he finished, a little boy not more than nine years old stepped out of a back pew, where he was sitting with his mother, and, going up to the clergyman, held out his hand for the plate. The clergyman gravely gave it to him, and the child, without the slightest sign of shyness, went about the church collecting the offerings of the congregation. This being done, he, with equal un-self-consciousness, gave the plate again to the clergyman and returned to his seat beside his mother.

"Did you tell him to do it?" I inquired of the mother, later.

"Oh, no," she answered; "he asked me if he might. He said he knew how, he saw it done every Sunday, and he was sure the minister would let him."

American children of the present day are surer than the children of any other nation have ever been that their fathers and their mothers and their ministers will allow them liberty to do in church, as well as with respect to going to church, such things as they know how to do, and eagerly wish to do. In our national love and reverence for childhood we willingly give the children the great gift that we give reluctantly, or not at all, to grown people - the liberty to worship God as they choose.

CONCLUSION

We are a child-loving nation; and our love for the children is, for the most part, of the kind which Dr. Henry van Dyke describes as "true love, the love that desires to bestow and to bless." The best things that we can obtain, we bestow upon the children; with the goodliest blessings within our power, we bless them. This we do for them. And they, - is there not something that they do for us? It seems to me that there is; and that it is something incalculably greater than anything we do, or could possibly do, for them. More than any other force in our national life, the children help us to work together toward a common end. A child can unite us into a mutually trustful, mutually cordial, mutually active group when no one else conceivably could.

A few years ago, I was witness to a most striking example of this. I went to a "ladies' day" meeting of a large and important men's club that has for its object the study and the improvement of municipal conditions. The city of the club has a nourishing liquor trade. The club not infrequently gives over its meetings to discussions of the "liquor problem"; - discussions which, I have been told, had, as a rule, resolved themselves into mere argumentations as to license and no-license, resulting in nothing. By some accident this "ladies' day" meeting had for its chief speaker a man who is an ardent believer in and supporter of no-license. For an hour he spoke on this subject, and spoke exceedingly well. When he had finished, there ensued that random play of question and answer that usually follows the presiding officer's, "We are now open to discussion." The chief speaker had devoted the best efforts of his mature life to bringing about no-license in his home city; the subject was to him something more than a topic for a discussion that should lead to no practical work in the direction of solving the "liquor problem" in other cities. He tried to make that club meeting something more vital than an exchange of views on license and no-license. With the utmost earnestness, he attempted to arouse a living interest in the "problem," and, of course, to make converts to his own belief as to the most effective solution of it.

Finally, some one said, "Isn't *any* liquor sold in your city? Your law keeps it from being sold publicly, but privately, - how about that?"

"I cannot say," the chief speaker replied. "The law may occasionally be broken, - I suppose it is. But," he added, "I can tell you this, - we have no drunkards on our streets. I have a boy, - he is ten years old, and he has never seen a drunken man in his life. How about the boys of the people of this city, of this audience?"

The persons in that audience looked at the chief speaker; they looked at each other. There followed such a serious, earnest, frank discussion of the "liquor problem" as had never before been held either in that club, or, indeed, in any assembly in that city. Since that day, that club has not only held debates on the "liquor problem" of its city; it has tried to bring about no-license. The chief speaker of that meeting was far from being the first person who had addressed the organization on that subject; neither was he the first to mention its relation to childhood and youth; but he was the very first to bring his own child, and to bring the children of each and every member of the association who had a child into his argument. With the help of the children, he prevailed.

One of my friends who is a member of that club said to me recently, "It was the sincerity of the speaker of that 'ladies' day' meeting that won the audience. I really must protest against your thinking it was his chance reference to his boy!"

"But," I reminded him, "it was not until he made that 'chance reference' to his boy that any one was in the least moved. How do you explain that?"

"Oh," said my friend, "we were not sure until then that he was in dead earnest -"

"And then you were?" I queried.

"Why, yes," my friend replied. "A man doesn't make use of his child to give weight to what he is advocating unless he really does believe it is just as good as he is arguing that it is."

"So," I persisted, "it *was*, after all, his 'chance reference' to his boy -"

"If you mean that nothing practical would have come of his speech, otherwise, - yes, it was!" my friend allowed himself to admit.

Another friend who happened to be present came into the conversation at this point. "Suppose he had had no child!" she suggested. "Any number of perfectly sincere persons, who really believe that what they are advocating is just as good as they argue it is, have no children," she went on whimsically; "what about them? Haven't they any chance of winning their audiences when they speak on no-license, - or what not?"

Those of us who are in the habit of attending "welfare" meetings of one kind or another, from the occasional "hearings" before various committees of the legislature, to the periodic gatherings of the National Education Association, and the National Conference of Charities and Correction, know well that, when advocating solutions of social problems as grave as and even graver than the "liquor problem," the most potent plea employed by those speakers who are not fathers or mothers begins with the words, "You, who have children." My friend who had said that a man did not make use of his child to give weight to his arguments unless he had a genuine belief in that for which he was pleading might have gone further; he might have added that neither do men and women make such a use of other people's children excepting they be as completely sincere, - provided that those men and women love children. And we are a nation of child-lovers.

It is because we love the children that they do for us so great a good thing. It is for the reason that we know them and that they know us that we love them. We know them so intimately; and they know us so intimately; and we and they are such familiar friends! The grown people of other nations have sometimes, to quote the old phrase, "entered into the lives" of the children of the land; we in America have gone further; - we have permitted the children of our nation to enter into our lives. Indeed, we have invited them; and, once in, we have not deterred them from straying about as they would. The presence of the children in our lives, - so closely near, so intimately dear! - unites us in grave and serious concerns, - unites us to great and significant endeavors; and unites us even in smaller and lighter matters, - to a pleasant neighborliness one with another. However we may differ in other particulars, we are all alike in that we are tacitly pledged to the "cause" of children; it is the desire of all of us that the world be made a more fit place for them. And, as we labor toward the fulfillment of this desire, they are our most effectual helpers.

In our wider efforts after social betterment, they help us. Because of them, we organize ourselves into national, and state, and municipal associations for the furtherance of better living, - physical, mental, and moral. Through them, we test each other's sincerity, and measure each other's strength, as social servants. In our wider efforts this is true. Is it not the case also when the field of our endeavors is narrower?

Several years ago, I chanced to spend a week-end in a suburban town, the population of which is composed about equally of "old families," and of foreigners employed in the factory situated on the edge of the town. I was a guest in the home of a minister of the place. Both he and his wife believed that the most important work a church could do in that community was "settlement" work. "Home-making classes for the girls," the minister's wife reiterated again and again; and, "Classes in citizenship for the boys," her husband made frequent repetition, as we discussed the matter on the Saturday evening of my visit.

"Why don't you have them?" I inquired.

"We have no place to have them in," the minister replied. "Our parish has no parish-house, and cannot afford to build one."

"Then, why not use the church?" I ventured.

"If you knew the leading spirits in my congregation, you would not ask that!" the minister exclaimed.

"Have you suggested it to them?" I asked.

"Suggested!" the minister and his wife cried in chorus. "*Suggested!*"

"I have besought them, I have begged them, I have implored them!" the minister continued. "It was no use. They are conservatives of the strictest type; and they cannot bring themselves even to consider seriously a plan that would necessitate using the church for the meeting of a boys' political debating club, or a girls' class in marketing."

"Churches are so used, in these days!" I remarked.

"Yes," the minister agreed; "but not without the sympathy and cooeperation of the leading members of the congregation!"

That suburban town is not one to which I am a frequent visitor. More than a year passed before I found myself again in the pleasant home of the minister. "I must go to my Three-Meals-a-Day Club," my hostess said shortly after my arrival on Saturday afternoon. "Wouldn't you like to go with me?"

"What is it, and where does it meet?" I asked.

"It is a girls' housekeeping class," answered the minister's wife; "and it meets in the church."

"The church?" I exclaimed. "So the 'leading spirits' have agreed to having it used for 'settlement' work! How did you win them over?"

"We didn't," she replied; "they won themselves over, - or rather the little children of one of them did it."

When I urged her to tell me how, she said, "We are invited to that 'leading spirit's' house to dinner to-morrow; and you can find out for yourself, then."

It proved to bean easy thing to discover. "I am glad to see that, since you have no parish-house, you are using your church for parish-house activities," I made an early occasion to say to our hostess, after dinner, on the Sunday. "You were not using it in that way when I was here last; it is something very new, isn't it?"

"It is, my dear," said our hostess, - one of those of his flock whom the minister had described as "conservatives of the strictest type"; "'very new' are the exact words with which to speak of it!"

"How did it happen?" I asked.

She smiled. "Our minister and his wife declare that my small son and daughter are mainly responsible for it!" she said. "They began to attend the public school this autumn, - they had, up to that time, been taught at home. You know what the population of this town is, - half foreign. Even in the school in this district, there are a considerable number of foreigners. I don't know why it is, when they have so many playmates in their own set, that my children should have made friends, and such close friends, with some of those foreign children! But they did. And not content with bringing them here, they wanted to go to their homes! Of course, I couldn't allow that. I explained to my boy and girl as well as I was able; I told them those people did not know how to live properly; that they might keep their children clean, because they wouldn't be permitted to send them to school unless they did; but their houses were dirty, and their food bad. And what do you think my children said to me? They said, 'Mother, have they *got* to have their houses dirty? Have they *got* to have bad food? Couldn't *they* have things nice, as *we* have?' It quite startled me to hear my own children ask me such things; it made me think. I told my husband about it; it made him think, too. You know, we are always hearing that, if we *are* going to try to improve the living conditions of the poor, we must 'begin with the children,' - begin by teaching them better ways of living. Our minister and his wife have all along been eager to teach these foreign children. We have no place to teach them in, except our church. It was rather a wrench for my husband and me, - giving our approval to using a church for a club-house. But we did it. And we secured the consent of the rest of the congregation, - we told them what our children had said. We were not the only ones who thought the children had, to use an old-fashioned theological term, 'been directed' in what they had said!" she concluded.

The children had said nothing that the minister had not said. Was it not less what they had said than the fact of their saying it that changed the whole course of feeling and action in that parish?

On the days when it is our lot to share in doing large tasks, the children help us. What of the days which bring with them only a "petty round of irritating concerns and duties?" Do they not help us then, too?

In a house on my square, there lives a little girl, three years old, who, every morning at about eight o'clock, when the front doors of the square open, and the workers come hurrying down their steps, appears at her nursery window, - open except in very stormy weather. "Good-bye!" she calls to each one, smiling, and waving her small hand, "good-bye!"

"Good-bye!" we all call back, "good-bye!" We smile, too, and wave a hand to the little girl. Then, almost invariably, we glance at each other, and smile again, together. Thus our day begins.

We are familiar with the thought of our devotion to children. As individuals, and as a nation, our services to the children of our land are conspicuously great. "You do so much for children, in America!" It is no new thing to us to hear this exclamation. We have heard, we hear it so often! All of us know that it is true. We are coming to see that the converse is equally true; that the children do much for us, do more than we do for them; do the best thing in the world, - make us who are so many, one; keep us, who are so diverse, united; help us, whether our tasks be great or small, to "go to our labor, smiling."

Choose from Thousands of 1stWorldLibrary Classics By

Adolphus WilliamWard
Aesop
Agatha Christie
Alexander Aaronsohn
Alexander Kielland
Alexandre Dumas
Alfred Gatty
Alfred Ollivant
Alice Duer Miller
Alice Turner Curtis
Alice Dunbar
Ambrose Bierce
Amelia E. Barr
Andrew Lang
Andrew McFarland Davis
Anna Sewell
Annie Besant
Annie Hamilton Donnell
Annie Payson Call
Anton Chekhov
Arnold Bennett
Arthur Conan Doyle
Arthur Ransome
Atticus
B. M. Bower
Basil King
Bayard Taylor
Ben Macomber
Booth Tarkington
Bram Stoker
C. Collodi
C. E. Orr
C. M. Ingleby
Carolyn Wells
Catherine Parr Traill
Charles A. Eastman
Charles Dickens
Charles Dudley Warner
Charles Farrar Browne
Charles Ives
Charles Kingsley
Charles Lathrop Pack
Charles Whibley
Charles Willing Beale
Charlotte M. Braeme
Charlotte M.Yonge
Clair W. Hayes
Clarence Day Jr.
Clarence E. Mulford

Clemence Housman
Confucius
Cornelis DeWitt Wilcox
Cyril Burleigh
D. H. Lawrence
Daniel Defoe
David Garnett
Don Carlos Janes
Donald Keyhole
Dorothy Kilner
Dougan Clark
E. Nesbit
E.P.Roe
E. Phillips Oppenheim
Edgar Allan Poe
Edgar Rice Burroughs
Edith Wharton
Edward J. O'Biren
John Cournos
Edwin L. Arnold
Eleanor Atkins
Elizabeth Cleghorn
Gaskell
Elizabeth Von Arnim
Ellem Key
Emily Dickinson
Erasmus W. Jones
Ernie Howard Pie
Ethel Turner
Ethel Watts Mumford
Eugenie Foa
Eugene Wood
Evelyn Everett-Green
Everard Cotes
F. J. Cross
Federick Austin Ogg
Ferdinand Ossendowski
Francis Bacon
Francis Darwin
Frances Hodgson Burnett
Frank Gee Patchin
Frank Harris
Frank Jewett Mather
Frank L. Packard
Frederick Trevor Hill
Frederick Winslow Taylor
Friedrich Kerst
Friedrich Nietzsche
Fyodor Dostoyevsky

Gabrielle E. Jackson
Garrett P. Serviss
Gaston Leroux
George Ade
Geroge Bernard Shaw
George Ebers
George Eliot
George MacDonald
George Orwell
George Tucker
George W. Cable
George Wharton James
Gertrude Atherton
Grace E. King
Grant Allen
Guillermo A. Sherwell
Gulielma Zollinger
Gustav Flaubert
H. A. Cody
H. B. Irving
H. G. Wells
H. H. Munro
H. Irving Hancock
H. Rider Haggard
H. W. C. Davis
Hamilton Wright Mabie
Hans Christian Andersen
Harold Avery
Harold McGrath
Harriet Beecher Stowe
Harry Houidini
Helent Hunt Jackson
Helen Nicolay
Hendy David Thoreau
Henrik Ibsen
Henry Adams
Henry Ford
Henry Frost
Henry James
Henry Jones Ford
Henry Seton Merriman
Henry Wadsworth
Longfellow
Henry W Longfellow
Herbert A. Giles
Herbert N. Casson
Herman Hesse
Homer
Honore De Balzac

Horace Walpole
Horatio Alger, Jr.
Howard Pyle
Howard R. Garis
Hugh Lofting
Hugh Walpole
Humphry Ward
Ian Maclaren
Israel Abrahams
J.G.Austin
J. Henri Fabre
J. M. Barrie
J. Macdonald Oxley
J. S. Knowles
J. Storer Clouston
Jack London
Jacob Abbott
James Allen
James Lane Allen
James Andrews
James Baldwin
James DeMille
James Joyce
James Oliver Curwood
James Oppenheim
James Otis
Jane Austen
Jens Peter Jacobsen
Jerome K. Jerome
John Burroughs
John F. Kennedy
John Gay
John Glasworthy
John Habberton
John Joy Bell
John Milton
John Philip Sousa
Jonathan Swift
Joseph Carey
Joseph Conrad
Joseph Jacobs
Julian Hawthrone
Julies Vernes
Justin Huntly McCarthy
Kakuzo Okakura
Kenneth Grahame
Kate Langley Bosher
L. A. Abbot
L. T. Meade
L. Frank Baum
Laura Lee Hope

Laurence Housman
Leo Tolstoy
Leonid Andreyev
Lewis Carroll
Lilian Bell
Lloyd Osbourne
Louis Tracy
Louisa May Alcott
Lucy Fitch Perkins
Lucy Maud Montgomery
Lydia Miller Middleton
Lyndon Orr
M. H. Adams
Margaret E. Sangster
Margaret Vandercook
Maria Edgeworth
Maria Thompson Daviess
Mariano Azuela
Marion Polk Angellotti
Mark Overton
Mark Twain
Mary Austin
Mary Cole
Mary Rowlandson
Mary Wollstonecraft
Shelley
Max Beerbohm
Myra Kelly
Nathaniel Hawthrone
O. F. Walton
Oscar Wilde
Owen Johnson
P.G.Wodehouse
Paul and Mable Thorn
Paul G. Tomlinson
Paul Severing
Peter B. Kyne
Plato
R. Derby Holmes
R. L. Stevenson
Rabindranath Tagore
Rahul Alvares
Ralph Waldo Emmerson
Rene Descartes
Rex E. Beach
Richard Harding Davis
Richard Jefferies
Robert Barr
Robert Frost
Robert Gordon Anderson
Robert L. Drake

Robert Lansing
Robert Michael Ballantyne
Robert W. Chambers
Rosa Nouchette Carey
Ross Kay
Rudyard Kipling
Samuel B. Allison
Samuel Hopkins Adams
Sarah Bernhardt
Selma Lagerlof
Sherwood Anderson
Sigmund Freud
Standish O'Grady
Stanley Weyman
Stella Benson
Stephen Crane
Stewart Edward White
Stijn Streuvels
Swami Abhedananda
Swami Parmananda
T. S. Ackland
The Princess Der Ling
Thomas A. Janvier
Thomas A Kempis
Thomas Anderton
Thomas Bailey Aldrich
Thomas Bulfinch
Thomas De Quincey
Thomas H. Huxley
Thomas Hardy
Thomas More
Thornton W. Burgess
U. S. Grant
Valentine Williams
Victor Appleton
Virginia Woolf
Walter Scott
Washington Irving
Wilbur Lawton
Wilkie Collins
Willa Cather
Willard F. Baker
William Makepeace
Thackeray
William W. Walter
Winston Churchill
Yei Theodora Ozaki
Young E. Allison
Zane Grey

www.ingramcontent.com/pod-product-compliance
Lightning Source LLC
Chambersburg PA
CBHW022116280326
41933CB00007B/416